A SAFARI GUIDE'S TALES FROM ZIMBABWE

The Zambezi Valley, Matusadona and Mana Pools

GAVIN FORD

June '16

Dear and Estrella —
The "quiet couple" whose quiet
perception belies their acuity of understanding.

Gavin

Print information available on the last page

Rev. date: 05/13/2015

To order additional copies of this book, contact:
Xlibris
0800-056-3182
www.xlibrispublishing.co.uk
Orders@ Xlibrispublishing.co.uk

CONTENTS

SMALL BEGINNINGS

I have been guiding safaris since 1982, and prior to that, I had spent an amazingly free youth, growing up in a typical, English-speaking family in Eastern Rhodesia, now Zimbabwe. My father divorced my mother in 1971, when I was fifteen. He had been a career soldier since 1938, enlisting at the outbreak of WW2 and going on to fight through the European and Far Eastern battlefields. Dad was awarded the Military Cross for 'gallantry in the field' and later an MBE for his work with soldiers and their families in the post-war period. My father moved the family down from Kenya, to Zambia, and eventually to Rhodesia in the heady days when opportunities offered themselves in abundance here. Travelling in an old army landrover and a Vauxhall station wagon my parents had brought us three kids and two dogs down, over the newly built Kariba dam wall, to settle initially in Salisbury (then) and then on to Umtali. It was here that we finally settled and they never moved again. My two older sisters and I attended the local high schools, and they moved away to live their lives elsewhere in the country.

When Dad moved out and married again, he lived in Mutare for the remainder of his life, and I had a rather regrettably distant relationship with him, until his death in 2007.

Mother and I lived in a couple of great 'out of the way' houses until I was eighteen. She had encouraged each one of us in our interests and my sisters, Russett and Pixie became very accomplished horse women. Both achieving a degree of notoriety in different fields of the horse world, from playing provincial Polo-X, and show jumping to finally running the remount section for the mounted infantry unit, The Grays Scouts in the final stages of the Rhodesian bush war!

My mother was always interested in what I was doing and never complained about the snakes, crocodiles, birds and other fascinating bits of natural history that I would bring back from my walks and jaunts into the bush. She herself had had an interest in wild creatures as a child growing up in rural Basingstoke, England. She had encouraged me to pursue what had started at a very young age, a deep and passionate interest in 'the bush'. It was to prove a lifelong affair and lasts to this day, having provided me with a way of life and career for more than 36 years!

After my final school exams, I left home and rode off into the early morning rain on an old BSA Golden Flash motorbike on a journey around the country through all the rural areas before the liberation war really gathered momentum and destroyed the peace and goodwill in the country.

Umtali (now Mutare) was my 'home town', and of course, Umtali Boys High School was where I completed my secondary education. Located where we were, many of us, after completing stints in the armed forces, which was mandatory at that time (and we went willingly), became involved in some ways in the wildlife industry. To this day, there are at least a dozen individuals whose livelihoods are earned through the tourism or wildlife sector, all from the border town of Umtali. It was the prettiest little country town in the basin between two mountain ranges with a wonderful community spirit.

Rhodesia was a fantastic, free, and invigorating country to grow up in, and we loved it. To this day, most Zimbabweans who now live in foreign countries will talk about 'home' and how they loved it. Their hearts still dwell in this wonderful tortured country, and there is a strong urge to return. Many will, in time, or their children will.

The onset of our stand against communist-backed politics came to a head in 1965, and we went to war against a brutal and vengeful terrorist army through Mozambique and Zambia. This culminated in the independence in 1980, and this wonderful country, after an initial honeymoon period of fifteen years, has seen the results of our worst fears in the last decades under Robert Mugabe and his ZANU-PF party.

Today, in Zimbabwe, a very different environment is apparent for young adults of all races and origins to grow in. More than three million Zimbabweans are estimated to have left the country of their birth and spread far and wide across the planet, starting new lives far from their ancestors, their families and aged parents, and their history. Today they comprise the diaspora, the unseen 'nation', and, until recently, the source of foreign currency to Zimbabwe. This changed when the Zimbabwe government, prior to the joint government formation, illegally adopted the United States dollar as its official currency.

GUIDING IN ZIMBABWE – THE EARLY 1980S

The Zambezi Valley has charisma. If you have drunk its water and walked the dusty trails created by generations of elephants and wildlife, you will understand.

I spent fifteen years of my career walking the original game trails of 'The Valley' and forging new routes through its woodlands and thickets, drinking water from ancient secret springs. The Zambezi Valley from Chizarira; the Matusadona National Park, Kariba; Kariba Gorge to Chewore; and Mpata Gorge, inland to the dense woodlands of the Mkanga Bridge; and then Kanyemba was my stamping ground, and I have canoed that mighty river from Kariba to Kanyemba many, many times.

Mana Pools became a byword in Zimbabwean households and, together with Hwange National Park, formed two very popular holiday parks for a lucky generation of Zimbabweans. Several safari operators started their careers in the parks, and fortunately, Rhodesian national parks were run by forward-thinking and very smart individuals in those days, with a sincere commitment rarely observed today. We were fortunate to have a freedom not seen even in the parks of our neighbouring countries to this day, and despite the negative political situation in the country, we, as licensed professional guides, still are allowed that same freedom and are allowed to own and carry firearms in the course of our tourist activities. Truly, an anomaly in a country ruled by paranoia.

Having now travelled extensively in Africa for thirty plus years, guiding and leading safaris throughout East Africa, Gabon, Zambia, Namibia, and Botswana too, I think guides still have the best opportunities for training and learning the 'real' business in Zimbabwe.

Along with a handful of old-school professional hunters and guides, I was fortunate to be directly involved in the process of creating the examination process and standards associated with that qualification which set the benchmark for guiding and hunting in the whole sub-region.

Zimbabwean professional guides have established a world-renowned reputation for professionalism to this day.

I was fortunate to have the opportunity to visit Hwange National Park as a guide in those early days as well, and so enjoyed the two areas intimately, but most of my experiences were in the Zambesi valley.

Of course, not every trail had charging lions or rhinos at all, but over the years, I accumulated a number of incidents, and I have put them down to share the sights and sounds that I am certain will have gone from the Zambezi Valley for good.

CHIKWENYA

Kazungula Safaris won the concession from national parks in 1982 and built Chikwenya camp on the old 'G' hunting campsite, at the junction of the Sapi and Zambezi rivers. Mana Pools National Park was across the Sapi River, normally a broad sandy expanse for eleven months of the year. In those early years, that bottom end of Mana was pretty wild and very rarely visited by anybody, and when we built Chikwenya camp, there were still areas that we were discovering for the first time as resident guides. John and Nicci Stevens were the first camp managers there, and together with Briar, their four-year-old daughter, they lived in a tent just fifty metres from the dining room area of Chikwenya. The area was idyllic and, in later years, nearly 30 per cent of our bookings were return guests.

I had just joined Fothergill Island as an assistant manager and was doing my hunting and guiding apprenticeship under Rob Fynn and Ura de Woronin. Gael, my wife, was the caterer, and Janet Conway (ex-nurse, fabulous hostess, and a fun person) was the receptionist. Rob and Sandy Fynn had built Fothergill Island camp during the late 1970s, the latter years of the Liberation War, as it is known in Zimbabwe. Fothergill Island was a dream safari camp, built by hand, and Rob was a pioneer way ahead of the competition. Time and circumstances eventually overtook Rob and Sandy, and they left the island when Sandy's deteriorating health forced them to leave.

Chikwenya had been built with a minimalist plan, according to national parks stipulations, and it was a wild, wonderful, and fabulous wildlife camp. The chalets all faced the river and were constructed of low, wire-clad walls (one metre high) under an A-frame thatched roof, simple wooden doors, cement floors, and open-roofed bathrooms, with a shower, loo, and handbasin. That was it.

In those years, it was considered to be one of the best wildlife destinations in the whole country. Mana is a National Park located on a section of the Zambezi river, where the great river has carved out swathes of the northern riverbank (Zambia), creating a floodplain on the south side of the river. Great layers of silt have been deposited over hundreds of years on the Zimbabwean side, creating a floodplain which has a woodland of towering winterthorn (or Apple-ring Acacia) trees. These trees are a vital part of the ecosystem of Mana because of their prolific and nutritious seed pods which cause a considerable movement of the elephants in the district, and other herds of browsers, to come down on to the floodplain, specifically to feed on the pods.

There are four significant 'oxbow' pools along the floodplain, ranging in size from a hundred metres to nearly two kilometres in extent. These are what gave Mana its name – 'mana' means four in the local Shona and Tonga dialect.

We had black rhino, elephant, lion, leopard, buffalo, nyala, and a host of other animals, which shared the bush, and we had the freedom to walk and to explore that whole area at will. It was incredible. It was a time that was to touch all of our lives forever, particularly the Stevens family. John and I became great friends and explored the area at length.

TRACKED BY AN ELEPHANT COW

It was whilst we were having a short break from Fothergill and staying at Chikwenya Camp that I decided to take a walk on Chikwenya Island and look for an albino bushbuck ram that had been seen there.

I had left my wife Gael in the small boat, which we had used to get up to the island in, moored on the bank. She was terrified of elephants and had no wish to walk there as the island had a large number of elephant cows and calves on it at the time. So I set off through the Natal mahogany and *Senna* spp. thickets where the bushbuck are normally found in numbers. I was not carrying a rifle at all, only a pair of binoculars and my camera, with a 70–300-mm zoom lens.

As I had expected, there were elephants scattered over the whole area, some bulls feeding quietly on the jesse and other plants, and cows too either standing in small groups or walking purposefully across the dusty plain to the river or from the shade trees to better feeding spots. I pushed on ever mindful of the wind direction and elephants. Skirting some thickets, I had seen two buffalo bulls dozing in the shade and carefully avoided showing myself and moved slowly towards the Zambian side of the island, scanning the jesse and clumps of *Capparis* for bushbuck feeding. The strongly scented blossoms were a favourite for bushbuck and impala here. I had seen a few ewes and one adult ram, but not the one I was looking for.

I had alternated between moving and scanning clumps of bush and after forty-five minutes or so was by now some distance down the island, constantly moving to avoid elephants and their young. Eventually, an uncomfortable feeling came over me, and I stopped and rested out of sight inside a jesse thicket.

I waited and watched, trying to find out what my sixth sense was warning me about. The sandy plains were beginning to heat up, and a small mirage was rising over the open areas. Elephants were beginning to group in lazy, ear-flapping, huddled groups under the winterthorn (*Faidherbia albida*). Impala stood about, browsing here and there, and their contented grunts and soft bleats came to me now and then. The bird song was quiet now in the heat; only the harsh, 'squeear' calls of the Meve's starlings and their continuous chatter emanated from the denser cover of the tall winterthorn and mahogany thickets. Here and there, an ear waggled in silhouette, as an impala or a bushbuck was bothered by flies.

Scanning on all sides of me, I noticed an elephant cow was moving slowly, but carefully, along the edge of the treeline, her trunk outstretched in front of her, just touching the ground with every second or third step. She had no calves with her, just her very intense concentration. She was totally fixed on her trunk, her ears slightly raised and her feet moving deliberately and silently . . . following the route I had taken. I watched her carefully, retracing my path through the edge of the thickets. There I had moved to the left to avoid a fallen thorn tree, around a termite mound past a *Balanites* tree with all its terrible long spines destroyed by elephants. I had crouched down crossing an open patch, moving slowly to avoid attention and scaring the impala . . . The elephant was now about sixty metres from me and heading inexorably to my patch.

I was suddenly nervous. I looked about me, and there was only jesse and some mahogany trees, too small to climb high enough out of reach.

I looked back again at her. Closer now . . . close enough for me to see her trunk tips hover over the ground, where I had had a pee minutes before, and the mud on her eyelashes clear in my view. Her thin, cow tusks one longer and clean and the other chipped a little stained with tree sap. My heart gave a little skip.

Suddenly, my legs moved, and I scuttled behind the bush for cover and to the edge of the river . . . downwind. Keeping out of sight, right on the edge of the riverbank, I started to back track, had to, as the wind was across us both. She was going to be about thirty metres to my left now, well within her visual range. I crouched down behind some dead, leafless *Senna* stems . . . some impala scattered and snorted the alarm . . . bounding away, across her front, and the dust drifted slowly towards my hiding place. The elephant started, her little piggy eyes staring, ears wide outspread. She was looking away from me at the impala . . . , watching them and assessing them with her elephant brain. I moved quickly past her and quietly. My adrenaline was flowing strongly now, my head was clearer, and my heart pounding, but everything was under control. She was behind me, not far, but behind me and moving away.

My bootlace caught a thorn branch and dragged behind me, rustling the dead stems and making a huge racket . . . damn. I bent down and my camera swung forward and hit me in the face, just on the cheek . . . hurt like hell. I looked back, and the elephant had stopped and was sniffing my last resting spot, her rounded body a quarter away from me. Her trunk tip touching and collecting my scent where I had stood, leant against the stems, and wiped my hands on the bark of the young *Diospyros* to rid myself of the sweaty feeling from the heat. Now I was sweating from fear.

She seemed to ignore the noise of the bushes I had just made . . . her muddy, stained, grey ears just seemed to rise a little higher . . .

Tearing my fingers on the curved thorns, I freed my shoelace and half-crouching and half-running with exaggerated quietness I moved on and away.

Each step was feeling better . . . I glanced back. She had stopped and was looking towards the river, her trunk raised testing the wind. I carried on and nearly walked straight into a cow and calf resting deep in a mahogany thicket. Her swinging tail and trunk-like legs had given her away. The very young calf lying between her legs . . . eyes closed. I paused for a fraction of a second and swung riverside, making a noise as I did so the cow swung around, startled by the proximity of the noise, but was unwilling to leave her young calf, thank goodness.

I didn't stop, but skidded down the bank above the green water of the deep river channel. My feet sliding in the loose sand . . . I kept going, grabbing a root as thick as my wrist and praying that it was going to hold. The bank was too steep now, I had to go up . . . my luck was in. There was a clear patch and then clumps of *Capparis* thickets and mahogany. Sweating profusely now and my camera full of sand, I crawled over the lip of the bank, sending cascades of sand into the river, alerting every crocodile within a hundred metres, I'm sure.

Ignoring the pain in my knees from the dreadful spines of the *Tribulus* seeds, I brushed and pulled them out, looking behind me as I walked. Scanning each possible buffalo hideout and shady spot, I moved into the shade and walked quickly through the woodland, welcoming the cover. Pausing and, again, looked behind me . . . a dark shadow brushed through the branches, and I heard soft cracking noises as the elephant followed me. Crouching down, I could see her legs walking steadily along the trail I had taken. She was still following her trunk, although I was essentially just still within her visual range if it had been open.

I had to move faster. I knew more or less where I was, and the last thing I needed was to lead her back to the boat, where matters would only get far worse. I started to jog, following an elephant trail, cleared of leaves and debris by animals using it, through the mahogany trees and small clearings. I could see the other side of the island now and the far bank of the mainland. The clearings got bigger now, and then I found a huge 'winterthorn' with an old, thick *Capparis* creeper hanging from it. Swinging my camera behind my back, I climbed easily about ten metres up it, managing to clamber on to the main branch, skinning my legs and thighs on the rough bark as I did so.

I waited, feeling a lot safer . . . high enough from her trunk and her rage, if she chose to vent it on the tree.

The starlings were quiet. Only the insects and cicadas were present. I waited.

As silently as a leopard, a big grey leopard, mind you, the cow emerged along the trail. The silence of her intensity was scary . . . I stared at her approaching mass, the wrinkles on her sway back fine, and stretched across the broadest part of her barrel. Her shoulder skin, dusted with the reddish sand of the mainland jesse, moved rhythmically as she seemed to glide along the trail. The top of her head was wrinkled across its width and the back of her ears was smooth as rubber gloves. She did not see me . . . elephants very rarely look up, even though they are quite capable of this movement.

She walked past the creeper a few strides, her trunk questing and touching the ground searching. I waited, wide-eyed and still, mouth dry. She stopped . . . Her trunk searching still, swinging around behind her sideways, finding, she stepped back and swung to the creeper. I got a lot thinner on top of the branch . . . It was a thick branch though. Waited . . . not breathing.

Silence – I peered sideways, carefully. Her trunk tips were apart, moist and dusty, touching, tentative, sucking in all of my scent where I had hugged the creeper as I clambered up it. She smelt the creeper, all the way up and then swung, flare-eared around, head raised, looked. Those coffee-brown eyes, stared wide, white-ringed and searching for what? Did she know what I was? Did she have an age-old score to settle? The main thing was she didn't comprehend *where* I was right then. She swung first to one side and then the other, staring, her tusks jutting forward, head raised. My scent would have been strong and heavily tinged with fear. Animals always know fear, and she had scared me. She shook her head, irritated. Dust blew about her.

I breathed slowly, stuttering at the effort. I needed to pee. She let her trunk fall idly to the ground, extending it, the muscles slowly relaxed. The tip twitched in the dust, the moistness collecting in little wet stains. Standing there, her ears still tense but half-open . . . her eyes still open, expectant, and wary. I suppose it was only five to eight minutes before she moved. Slowly, she shifted, moved away from the creeper, her trunk still touching it, leaving a small trace of dribble on its bark.

Some impala walked innocently out into the clearing, and she swung up and stared at them. They ignored her and trotted past her, unafraid but slightly alarmed by her attitude.

Another few minutes . . . , by now, I was really desperate . . . , sweat had soaked my shirt and my hat. My binocular strap was slippery and uncomfortable. My camera gritty and sticky with sweat. I watched her closely. Her eyes started to droop and relax. I waited. She stood. I shifted and brushed ants off my legs. Urine has a strong scent, and I really didn't fancy getting her attention, *but* . . .

Eventually, a small group of cows rumbled from within the woodland. That lovely deep resonance carried clearly through the heat of the midday. The cow stirred and swayed, and almost reluctantly, slowly walked away into the trees. I shifted and 'caterpillared' along the branch to the main trunk, stood up shakily, had a pee. I took a series of deep breaths and waited until some confidence returned.

I walked to the creeper and with considerable difficulty managed to get a grip on the broad, roughened bark and very carefully climbed halfway down, scanning the woodland into which the cow had disappeared. Coast clear? Yes, down I went and walked rapidly towards where I had left the boat, walking upriver first to keep my scent away from the cows. Within ten minutes, I reached the boat and Gael. She looked at me curiously. 'Well, what happened. You look strained?'

'Let's get on to the river, and I'll tell you.'

'Elephants?'

I nodded. 'OK, let's get outa here!'

That incident was the only time I ever experienced such focus and intensity from an elephant or, in fact, any large mammal on my scent. She taught me a very valuable lesson that day, and fortunately, I survived to write about it. Yet I cannot even say she was after me with evil intent, as I have had elephant follow me for long distances since then, and without any drama, have let them approach me to close range (I was visual, behind a large fallen tree) without any aggression. They were just curious, I suppose. But as a young trainee guide it scared the hell out of me then, and I have not taken any chances with a cow elephant again.

Many years later, I had a square-lipped rhino in Hwange follow my scent for some distance, but she never found us on our walk, but I do know that she created problems with another guide who used to walk in that area. I have also had both black and white rhino bulls follow the sound of our voices and close with us, both occasions were during breaks in our drives and walks. The black rhino ran off after I shouted at him, and we escaped in a vehicle from the white rhino. He already had one vehicle to his credit.

RONNIE, THE RHINO

Once whilst Gael and I were spending a few days in Chikwenya camp during a quiet spell and were going out after lunch, I happened to see a rhino right at John's tent. Curious, I walked closer and watched in amazement as this young rhino put his nose down to sniff Briar's toy trunk at the foot of her bed, and then lift it up and down several times. The lid clanging every time. John and Nicci were resting a few metres away in the same tent at the time.

He continued to do this for several minutes until growing tired of it, he stood in the entrance for a few minutes and then gradually moved away to browse on the *Flueggea* and *Diospyros bushes* growing nearby.

John christened him Ronnie. Ronnie became so used to the staff at the camp that he would doze off in the shade of a bush right next to the kitchen door, totally ignoring the staff walking in and out carrying food and all their chatter as they prepared food for the day. The entrance posts holding the thatch wall of the totally open-air dining room were two of his favourite scratching posts, and he would amble through at anytime, scratch himself on one side and then the other before walking between the tables and benches and taking himself away. The two posts remained pushed outwards until the camp was rebuilt in early 1999.

I would delight in sitting not far from Ronnie and watch him snooze in the shade of the jesse.

He would spend ages just standing and staring into the distance before rather awkwardly lying down and shifting his weight, and making himself comfortable. Then he would sigh deeply, blowing through his nose and creating little dust storms with each nostril. His ears would wag individually, and then as he lost consciousness, they would twitch and work independently, facing this way and that at any intruding noise. He would sleep soundly when it was really hot and then wander down to the nearby muddy creek for a mudbath on the edge of the flood plain. An early morning walk would find him munching with closed eyes in his favourite patch of Crocodile bark or Acorn Diospyros, the loud crunching giving him away from at least a hundred metres. One morning, John and I found nine rhinos around the airfield at Chikwenya in the Puna jesse, in under an hour. Surely, a record worth mentioning in today's historical perspective.

Ronnie died one season of natural causes, and we found his dried out hide and bones intact not far from the river on the edge of a thicket. He was the first of several animals who seemed to sense they were safe at Chikwenya in those early days of the camp. We had a bushbuck ram for two seasons called Notch (for the cut in his one ear) and several elephant bulls as well. They all disappeared after a while, back to the company of their own kind.

SUSIE

Two years later, when Jeff and Veronica Stutchbury had taken over the management of the camp, very ably assisted by Dave Winhal and Elspeth Bailey, we had another interesting rhino character come to stay for a while. Dave and I were on an afternoon game drive in the trusty old Land Rovers that we used to have at that time. Dave had taken the route up past what Jeff had called Grasshopper Creek, to an open area of old flood plain, and I was muddling around the edge of the flood plain along where there was an old fig tree, which was used by a leopard from time to time.

We never had radios in those days, so no inter-vehicular communication was possible.

If you broke down, you fixed it or walked back to the camp. If you got badly stuck, you extracted yourself, walked, or waited – simple.

I had completed my circuit and was driving slowly along the edge of the gulley towards the river when I saw Dave's vehicle in the middle of the grassland, and everybody was staring at something. I stopped and glassed the area. There in the patchy tall grass was a large rhino, with a decent front horn and blade-shaped long back horn that almost touched the front one.

Quickly, appraising my guests of this phenomenon, I drove through the gulley, responded to Dave's frantic arm-waving with a wave of my hat, and we slowly and quietly as possible drove the old Land Rover, wheezing and grinding up the slope towards the plain.

I parked some distance to the side of Dave's vehicle, and we both sat with our guests, spellbound by this incredible windfall of a sighting. We very rarely found rhino in the open like this. We talked in hoarse whispers describing what we were seeing, keeping the sound to the minimum. The sun beat down from over the Zambian escarpment, and the flies and fidgeting started. Someone needed a pee . . . OK. So I led the needy person to a scrubby bush ten metres behind the car. She finished. The rhino started to move towards us . . . quick, quick into the car, without making any noise. *Must not* scare the rhino. Everybody smiled at everybody. This was good.

Slowly, the rhino advanced towards us . . . then chewed on a bush. 'Can we take photographs . . . ?'

My dilemma . . . 'OK, just a few, then stop'. A short flurry of lenses focusing, sounding like sci-fi toys, whining in and out, and the rhino kept coming, now towards Dave's car. It was a cow, a female . . . , she plodded forwards. We stared in wonder and fascination. Rhino charged cars and damaged them. What to do?

I said, 'Get your cameras ready! Take a few shots, but put your lenses on manual. No noise!'

There was staccato of shutter sounds. (Remember these were *Film* times, not digital)

The rhino stopped. I held my hand up. *Stop*! Silence. Dave looked nervous and excited.

His guests were a mix of characters . . . some excited, others huddled and nervous. Two were clutching their hats over their faces. I had no idea what he was telling his guests. The brave ones were taking a close look through binoculars and whispering to others without these. The rhino moved on . . . closer now and head up. When a rhino lifts its head up, it has seen you, or it's taking a clearer look . . . She was about twenty metres from the front of Dave's Land Rover, Jeff's vehicle in fact. We stared. She stared. Silence . . . and someone sneezed. A terrible, bursting-to-get-out type sneeze, squeezed into a tiny high-pitched snort.

You could have heard a squirrel on a nut a hundred yards away. She didn't move. The tension was unbearable. Dave was huddled behind his steering wheel, hand on the ignition foot on the pedal – waiting. She lowered her head wearily, blew loudly through her nose and plodded forward . . . Dave froze, everybody stared. The rhino walked straight up to the front of his car and sniffed it . . . blowing rhino breath on to the bumper, just inches from the radiator grill. She snuffed and sniffed . . . and then rested her great head on the iron. Her chin rested on the bumper, her horn touching the metal of the grill. She sighed . . . We stared . . . fingers on camera buttons. I looked at Dave whose neck had lengthened about two feet, trying to see what the rhino was doing. They all had. What an incredible sight!

Here was a wild rhino with its chin on the bumper of our game drive car . . . 'Quick, take a photo somebody,' I whispered. They all did.

This was Suzie, and she was with us for two seasons only, before the rhino poachers claimed her and shot her to death as she fed quietly on the edge of the flood plain. Her bones and her great weather proof hide bleached and gradually weathered away on the edge of the lower flood plain over the next four years. Her axe-scarred skull was collected by the park's rangers and added to the grisly collection outside the park office in Mana Pools. I sincerely hope the poachers who shot her were themselves pursued and wounded by the parks rangers before being eaten by crocodiles whilst crossing back to Zambia. It was the least they deserved.

The Rhino wars are a part of Zimbabwean history, which I sincerely hope will be written about soon, before we all get to old to remember correctly the deeds of incredible heroism by a few dedicated individuals both within national parks and the police. The insidious corruption by prominent politicians still in power today, the blatant double standards exhibited by those new government officials, and the tragedy of the losses we were powerless to stop. In a few short years, between 1985 and 1990, the black rhino disappeared from the Zambezi Valley.

HAVE YOU EVER SEEN A BROADBILL?

During my years as a guide, I have had a number of notable individuals and incidents, which for various reasons have stayed in my memory. Most for good reasons and others not so. Very rarely the latter, I may add. However, one such fellow stands out, and I shall call him Chuck, which is naturally not his real name. He and his party were my guests on a combination of a Porter Safari and Chikwenya. He did *not* do well on the first section, and instead of being honest with himself and me, he created all manner of excuses. He actually could not take the heat . . . , but he found everything wrong with my camp instead. Now we were at Chikwenya.

When we arrived in Chikwenya, he was with his son and daughter and their respective partners, a group of five – fine. He was a New Yorker, short, stocky, and full of stories of what a wonderful 'ultra-light' fisherman he was. This he shared with both tables at dinner, one table as a captive audience, and the other because he was particularly brash, loud, and obnoxious. Jeff looked at me and said nothing; just raised his very bushy eyebrows. Veronica rattled the plates and nudged me as she walked past, 'He's your guest, do something.' I chose my moment between stories. 'Have you ever seen a Broadbill?'

He opened his mouth to reply, looked puzzled, and paused to think. 'No. Have I caught one . . . probably' was his rejoinder – loud mirth. 'What?' I returned, looking suitably surprised. (There was absolutely no reason at all that he might have seen one of Southern Africa's most difficult small brown birds to locate).

'Oh well, then,' I remarked, looking deliberately smug. There was a silence at the table. 'That's a pity . . . now that's a *really* special sighting, hey, Jeff?' I cast a look at Jeff, sitting half-listening to me on the other table. He turned to me and feigned ignorance. 'What did you say?' His fingers curling his beard. I said, 'Chuck here has never seen a broadbill.' I paused, letting this information sink in with a look at Jeff. 'Hell, Gavin, What have you been doing with your guests? Didn't you say you've been together for a week already?'

'Of course, there's a population right here,' I said cockily. Jeff's eyebrows met in the middle, 'Oh, really?' Finding broadbills in the Zambezi Valley was in those days, rather like finding a unicorn drinking at the birdbath.

Gaining momentum, I continued, 'Chuck here has seen and done *everything* . . . but never seen a broadbill!'

'Well, you had better try and show him one then,' he said.

'Good luck there.' He turned back to his table, smiling and stroking his beard.

'It's pretty dangerous, going into the jesse with the cow elephants and rhino too,' I added.

'Never mind, perhaps some other time.'

I tried to pacify him. He looked a bit put out, and his son started on him. 'Come on, Dad. You're not going to take this are you? What is a broadbill anyway, an animal?' I waited for Chuck to answer. He hadn't asked what it was either.

'It's a small, brown, very rarely seen bird.'

'Only a bird . . . ,' disgusted that a bird should be regarded in such terms.

'Well, that's not worth any effort. Pah.' He spat.

'Well, you know that even Jeff hasn't seen one. It's that rare. Anyway, it's nothing really,' I continued.

'You have done a lot of other things, though, and walked with lions and elephants too.' I had walked them into a herd of buffalos that were totally unconcerned about our presence, including a big bull that walked almost straight into us sitting in the open. I had to stand up and tell him to push off, we weren't lions.

Conversation lapsed and the rest of the guests started conversations with each other and the subject was lost in the chit-chat across the table.

Chuck was quiet. Coffee was brought, and we all moved over to the fire, enjoying the mellow feeling of a day well spent, and a tomorrow filled with good things. Some folk went off to bed. Goodnights were called, and Jeff and Dave started escorting folks to their cabins. Some remained, and the fire held our gazes for a while.

'OK', I said, 'let's talk about tomorrow. We can do a walk or a drive up towards the next river in Mana, the Chitembe. There's a fishing owl and lions up there which might be fun. What do you want to do?' I addressed the group. The youngsters looked at each other, at Chuck.

'OK, do you all want to relax and have a late rise and breakfast then?' I asked, eyebrows raised.

'No, I want to see a bredbill,' he spoke, looking me in the eye.

'A broadbill?'

'Yup, a damned broadbill, whatever it is. I wanna see one, and you are goin' to find one so I can say, "I've seen a broadbill."' The die was cast.

'Well,' I began, 'it's pretty dangerous in there, you know. Cow elephants, old buffalo, lions . . .'

'Then you'll be earning your daily cut then, won't you.' He smirked. His trump card.

Early the next morning we set off walking up the Sapi river bed, soft sand crunching as we walked up towards the sacred forest across the river. The air was cold, and I had a jersey on with my daypack, holding my water bottle, some apples, and a small medic kit.

My trusted .458 rested easily on my arm, and I had a full ammo pouch with ten rounds of A-square Monolithic and a couple of soft-nosed rounds too.

I had briefed everybody as we left camp on the safety aspects of this particular walk as we were going into a very tight cover with a chance that we would unintentionally disturb elephant cows, rhinos, buffaloes, and of course, lions, as well. We walked in silence . . . each alone with their thoughts. I found a break in the riverine thicket and waited a moment before heading up into the cover, making sure that there were no animals right there.

We waited in silence. Only crickets and other insects made a noise. I scanned the thickets from my knees, checking for elephant tails swinging, horns, and ears anything that might give an animal away.

This was a tricky place to be. I chose a game trail and walked slowly, maximising my acute hearing ability and keeping the pace slow to avoid noisy sticks and leaves underfoot. Thorns snagged shirts and scratched legs and arms. I taught them to pass branches back to each other. After twenty minutes or so, we stopped under a flowering wild mango. The brilliant orange blossoms attracting flocks of starlings, bulbuls, sunbirds, and

red-headed weavers too. The fallen flowers created a gold carpet beneath the generously spreading tree boughs. Off to our left, an elephant screamed and trumpeting sounded across a wide area. I listened, watching my group. 'It's OK, just an elephant.' We carried on, walking silently through the dry jesse. A bushbuck suddenly barked and bounded away, little grunts with each jump. My group jumped and looked unsmilingly nervous. We carried on.

Baboons barked and a domestic fight broke out in front of us . . . , loud screams and thrashing branches marked their location. 'Baboons.' I whispered to the first in line. The tension was building already, and we had just started. A tap on my shoulder. 'An elephant.' I looked behind us through the jesse . . . a grey shape was moving slowly among the blossoms. 'No. Warthog.' I smiled at the messenger. They nodded and smiled back. Please, how does a warthog become an elephant? 'For Pete's sake,' I thought, looking away to screen my face. The baboons took off at our approach, and then I got down to check the ground ahead. Impala often feed on the leaves and fruit baboons drop, and I didn't want a whole herd of impala scaring off every bit of wildlife we might see. There were two female bushbuck, mother and daughter, nervous and dainty, feeding delicately, mouths full of orange blossoms and leaves, cheeks bulging, eyes dark and bright. They paused at seeing me, quivering with nerves, and then the adult took off, tail fluffed up and white showing; she uttered a single muffled bark. I smiled and stood up.

I was scanning the trees now, looking for this almost-impossible-to-see bird and hoping for a miracle. Bloody broadbill. I walked on and chose a shady copse to seat everybody. We scanned assiduously. I described the habitat carefully, pointing out the likely spots, and its courtship behaviour. Birdcalls filled the morning. Periodically, a branch would crack as elephant fed around us.

The deep rumbles of 'elephant talk' also came to us, and I described what this was . . . The girls looked nervous. Chuck and his son were irritated, or was it nerves too? 'We've just got to keep our eyes open,' I reassured them. In the distance, a lion roared, a long way off in fact. They looked at me. 'Lion,' I said. Their eyes widened in alarm. 'Where? How far?' I waved a hand, far away. More branches crackled near by, and we crouched down to see. A buffalo bull was making his way down to the river to our right – noisy fellow. We watched him move, collecting bits of vegetation over his blunt old horns and scabby sparsely haired black hide. He didn't see us against the shadowy stumps, and the wind hardly stirred in here.

We moved on. It was about eight o'clock now, and the sun was well over the trees, heating up the air and bush. The birds were very busy now, and all manner of activity was around us. 'Perfect', I thought. I spotted a Livingstone's flycatcher and got all excited, pointing it out to them, telling them how lucky we were to see this bird. Other birds passed us, and it was a fine morning count . . . , but no broadbill. More elephant cows feeding off to one side, and once, we had moved away from a lone cow, which had walked a scarce ten metres away, intent on something in her elephant-mind. Twice we had stopped for loo breaks, and everybody was sweating, jackets long ago discarded and tied around waists. I was still scanning trees and likely spots, determined to find this wretched bird. We walked on, straight into a sleeping rhino.

He stayed sleeping, but the effect it had on everybody was not good. There was a hasty council of war between the youngsters. The father was on the receiving end, and this time he motioned to me. 'What's up?' I asked.

'This is too dangerous, and we want to go back.'

'We have hardly arrived, and it will get quieter,' I answered.

'Everybody's feeding and being active right now, except for Dozy, back there.' I indicated in the direction of the rhino.

'But look, I understand, let's try somewhere else anyway. OK?' They nodded in agreement. The girls were looking decidedly pinched, and the son flushed. Gone was all the bravado and rudeness. Chuck just shrugged. 'As long as we see this bredbill or whatever it is.'

'Broadbill.'

I turned the group away, and we headed towards the old river step, where a line of evergreen trees still survived along the bluff. Cautiously, as there were still a lot of elephants around, we traversed the trails towards the green bank. I pulled the group under a huge clump of jesse and made them sit for a while and rest. We sat for a while, and I offered water. It was only about 9.30 a.m., but the heat was rising steadily. A small group of nyala walked by. I spotted their ultra-cautious movement and pointed to the group. Chuck glanced at them briefly, looked at me. 'Nyala,' I whispered, *really* excited about them. I gave my binoculars to one of the girls, showing her where to look, trying to get some positive mileage from these wonderful animals . . . They were not commonly seen then. The russet-and-white-striped does and a young ram stepped slowly forward, ears swivelling at every noise, legs poised in mid-step, nibbling here and there at a spring shoot, until they were out of sight.

We waited a bit longer. Then I heard it. A curious little sound of a bird chirrup. Again, I stopped breathing . . . yes. I did hear it . . . the courtship call of a broadbill. Excitedly, I tried to get them to listen with me . . . difficult when the birds were active in a semi-riverine habitat. They did try, but none had a musical ear. 'OK,' I said, 'let's go and find it'. The bush was thick, and at times we had to crawl along on hands and knees . . . it was tricky. We were all scratched and bleeding too, from the wait-a-bit thorn through which buffalo and rhino had created a tunnel. Something big smelt us and crashed away to the right of me . . . I was in the lead. Buffalo, I imagine. Nice one, Ford, I thought, I hadn't even seen it. The baboons started again . . . this time the short staccato barks. Clearly, they had found a predator, lioness, or leopard.

Their barks and screams were harsh and definite. I turned around and said, 'Baboons, they've found something they don't like'.

The eyes looked at me, cheeks besmudged with a little dirt, leaves in the hair (the daughter).
'Like what?'

'Probably a leopard in here,' I answered too truthfully.

'F – – k', she said, a real expression this time. I smiled.

'It's OK. The baboons will keep him busy anyway, and they don't eat people from New York.'

'Smart arse,' I thought, she did not need to hear that.

Eventually, we reached a patch from where we could see up into the edge of a big mahogany, partially hidden by a mangosteen. I scanned the tree carefully, and I found it. There, sitting still on the branch, looking a little plain and brown and streaked, was a broadbill.

I grabbed Chuck and hauled him to me, pointing up into the tree. He was looking bloody. His shirt was torn on the sleeve, his ear was bleeding delicately where a hooked thorn had had a go at him, his cheek was scratched, a whiplash branch probably, his shirt was half out and his legs were scratched as well. Leaf-mould hung off the sparse hairs on his legs. He pulled out his Swarovski binoculars and tried to focus them . . . with one eyecup still 'in'. I helped him pull it out. The bird sat still, looking like a piece of tree. The others wanted to see. I gave them my binos and pointed it out to them . . . tracing the branch and the route to the bird. Nope . . . nobody could see it from here.

'OK, let's move . . .' I lead them away to a better spot, out of the suns direction. I looked again . . . the bird had moved. 'The bird's moved.' Silence. Disbelief was on everybody's faces.

'It's moved. I can't help that. Let's find it.'

I searched again, willing the little brown-streaked breast to appear. Nothing. I glanced over at the next clump of trees . . . something small and brown . . . 'Yes. I've got him'. Same procedure again . . . but this time dodging and weaving branches and no easy reference points to pinpoint the bird for them . . . I couldn't believe how they couldn't see it. 'Look, it's a small, brown, streaked bird, this big,' For the fourth time, I indicated with my fingers. 'Lurking on the branch looking like a piece of . . .' I searched my mind.

Suddenly, Chuck said, 'I've got a little brown bird, dirt-streaked chest, ummmm.' He drifted into uncertainty. I looked where he was looking, 'Yes, that's it,' I cried in relief, raising my voice. I smiled hugely. I was proud of this short fellow from New York.

'It hasn't got a big bill at all. It looks ordinary and dirty,' He was disappointed.

'That's a broadbill,' I answered triumphantly.

'That's him'. I grinned excitedly. He lowered the glasses and looked at me. 'That's what we came looking for?'

'Yes, isn't it amazing!'.

He shook his head and sat down on a log.

The others were still trying to find it and kept asking each other for directions. I tried to help them and eventually they saw it. The bird flew away. They were nonplussed. 'I thought it was going to be bigger, and more colourful than that.'

Disappointment was ingrained in the voice. 'Oh well,' I thought, 'we found it, and Jeff will never believe me.'

We walked out of the jesse and thickets to the Mopane woodlands. Here it was open and far less stressful to walk, but the tsetse fly made our lives miserable and bit us relentlessly. Slapping and muttering, it was a subdued crew who followed me into the camp for brunch. I didn't try to conceal my pleasure in finding the broadbill.

They all went off to freshen up before the meal.

Most of the camp had returned when they eventually came back, and by then, the news of our success had reached everybody's ears, even the waiters. Jeff came in, all smiles and hearty. 'So you did it. Congratulations'.

He asked me the story, and I gave him the gist of it all . . . He was totally impressed, as were the others. Other guests who were birdwatchers were flabbergasted that we had actually found the Holy Grail of birders there in the jesse and impenetrable-out-of-the-way, 'We-don't-walk-there' bush!

When Chuck and his family arrived, everyone gave them a round of applause. They brightened up considerably. By the end of brunch and several versions of the story, they were very cheerful.

By the end of dinner that evening, Chuck was almost leading the safari through the bush.

RHINO RUN

Regrettably, politics and greed have forever altered the status of Africa's rhino populations. There was a time when finding a rhino in the Zambezi Valley was not hard, and surprisingly, those of us who worked in these regions were careful not to disturb these great beasts during the course of our perambulations. I used to walk the trails of these mountains with a free heart, a heart that sang of the joy of living with these animals and watching them bumble about on their trails created over generations of time. At one time, I was fortunate to observe eight rhino at one time in close proximity around a waterhole high up in the mountains. The rhino would snort at each other or whine and raise their tails in a comical curl and urinate in great squirts in territorial defiance of each other before gradually wandering in opposite directions to disappear in the scrub and gulleys to feed.

I used to lead wilderness trails through the Matusadona National Park, and over the years, they were definitely my most favourite occupation. I used to conduct the trails for groups of up to six people at a time, and we would be out for up to seven days. Our only equipment was a backpack (I carried a ninety litre pack with twenty kilogram or so), comprising of food, water bottle, sleeping bag, rubber mat, plastic groundsheet, and a mosquito net, a length of strong nylon or cotton cord, and of course, several items of clothing.

My .458 rifle was always part of my equipment as was my medic pack, which fitted on to the top of my pack. The Matusadona is divided into two natural zones. The shoreline and flat hinterland which goes to the escarpment base from the lakeshore and the escarpment itself and which is composed of five roughly parallel ranges of ragged ridges or hills, lying on an E-W orientation – the result of faulting and upliftment during the formation of the Rift Valley.

The Matusadona means, 'the dung falls . . .', and having known these hills for thirty years, it may be alluding to the carpet of elephant dung on the elephant trails leading up the hills, or the effort involved in climbing these steep ranges in the daytime heat of the Zambezi Valley.

I was conducting a wilderness trail with two guests who were desperate to see black rhino in the wild. I shall call them Michael and Anne. He had done some fieldwork for WWF in the Far East and was having a break between assignments. She was a highly qualified English nurse. He was six-foot plus and spare, and she was possibly five foot five and of medium build. We had set off from the Ume river side of the park, and I was intent on traversing the top of the ridges, and crossing the park west to east and exiting at a point where the escarpment drops into the lake. All was well, and off we set.

The first two days was great, and we saw a good variety of antelope, from sable and eland (rarely seen in those days) buffalo, elephant and grysbuck plus some wonderful real estate. We had heard lion every single night in the distance. My guests were fun and fully appreciated the walk, and it was very tough going at times. We had to draw water from the secret springs that I had found at different times and the evening wash was limited to a flannel wipe down at the most. One learns to appreciate water on trail, and I made sure no water supply was ever fowled with soaps of any kind. Washing was always done away from the stream or spring.

The third afternoon we were traversing the 'Elephant Highway 1'. This was a wide game trail running along one of the most spectacular ridges of the front part of the escarpment, with Lake Kariba on the north side and more hills on the southern side. It was level and easy going. We made good time and were busy admiring the views when I spotted the grey backs of two rhino ahead on the edge of a hill which we were going to traverse on the north side. They were about 250 metres ahead of us, and there was a crosswind from the north-east, in our favour. They were tremendously excited, and we watched them through the binoculars for a few minutes whilst I outlined the plan to approach them.

It was a big cow and a large, possibly three- to-four-year-old calf.

Between us and the rhino was a small tree-covered knoll, just on the edge of the direct approach line from which we would be able to observe the rhino safely and at a distance without alerting them to our presence. We walked quietly up to the knoll and, carefully, removed our packs and boots, placing them on the ground where we would collect them after our viewing. I leaned my rifle against a sapling next to my pack too. The distance was about one hundred metres to the rhino, and we had a more or less clear view of them feeding noisily in the scrub. I walked them a few metres down the steep slope to get a better view and to avoid creating a silhouette. Michael had his camera ready, and I was trying to move some branches for him to take a photo. I did not want the oxpeckers on the rhino to see us and give the alarm, so we had taken extra care not to expose ourselves or move about too much, even though the knoll was well treed and densely covered in a scrub layer up to waist height. Slowly, I parted the few branches. Michael raised his camera. I waited . . . and waited. I looked at him; he was busy looking at the animals. 'Michael, take it quickly, the oxpeckers will see us . . .', I whispered urgently in his ear.

He fiddled with the camera, and raised it again . . . I waited. 'Take it now,' I urged him.

The wind had dropped and all was still. Suddenly, totally without warning, the cow lifted her huge horned head, alarmed and snorted, ears cocked forward.

She snorted again and charged straight along the ridge, towards our knoll. She covered the distance in seconds. I grabbed Michael, and we waited, Anne was right behind me. The rhino disappeared from sight. The next second, she came crashing through the top of the knoll and on to our packs . . . She was scarcely fifteen metres from us, partially hidden from view. I crouched down, watching her through the scrub.

I motioned for absolute silence and pushed Anne up the little tree next to us. She clung to the tree in terror, her eyes wide at the implications. She had not seen where the rhino was, but could hear her snorting and the calf 'mewing' in distress and fear. I pushed Michael to the ground, and stuffed him into a bush, headfirst. I waved my finger at him to say *'stay there!'* He was mute with concern.

The cow, surrounded by fresh human scent had now had found our gear and was busy 'destroying it' flinging the packs about, snorting and growling. She was as light on her feet as a polo pony, charging and slashing, snorting and frothing at the bush and anything in her way. Her eyes were bloodshot and crazy. The calf bumped her, and she spun on him, knocking him over, so he squealed, and she slashed at the packs again. I pushed Anne as far as I could up the tree; her legs were shaking . . . , so were mine.

The cow stopped moving . . . her three-toed hooves still amongst the dust and shed leaves of her fury. I picked up a stone and lobbed it to our right about ten metres away. The cow charged again, straight past us snorting great snorts of fury and ire, her body crushing small trees and bushes like a runaway vehicle. She carried on down the hillside, the calf on his mother's tail, her progress marked by crashing bushes and the sound of stones rolling down the hill. Anne fell out of the tree. Michael had his eyes closed and winced as the cow went past us . . . , my heart was pounding with the rush of the moment. Thank goodness, she had left us alone.

Wow . . . What a moment that was!

We gathered ourselves and our packs, which fortunately had not been torn but only pummelled and one water bottle had burst its lid.

My rifle had been flung away and the butt carried a gouge for years, until I eventually worked it out with fine sandpaper and oil. Their cameras had been in their hands. Minimum damage . . . We were very lucky. We sat down, and I made tea. 'Bloody hell', Michael said, 'that was close!' An unnecessary observation, but we agreed. Anne had recovered her composure after a little weep and was sipping her tea quietly. Our adrenaline systems had worked overtime, and it was several minutes and much chatter to calm down. It was a nerve-racking experience, and not one that I ever wanted to repeat.

Nervous laughter and exaggerated smiles gave away our tension. Michael never took the photograph either. It was the closest brush I ever had with an aggressive rhino.

Eventually, we collected our gear, boots, and all and carried on to my night spot, an hour's walk hence. Our senses were now acute and progress was slow as every thicket was closely scrutinised for signs of *any* animal larger than a bushbuck. We had had enough adrenalin in our systems for today.

That evening we had camped at 'Trig Point' Spring. This wonderful generous spring was at the base of the hill, on a false crest of the slope beneath a tall jackal berry tree growing out of a large termite mound. It was a very well-used watering point for elephant, rhino, lion, buffalo bulls, and a host of smaller creatures and birds. The one side of the termite mound had been eaten away by game as it was a source of mineral salts. Lion had been close this evening, and we had seen them on the far hill, roaring into the dusk.

LIONS BY FIRELIGHT

The next day was our descent day, and we had a lazy morning. The lions had been active during the night, and I had not slept well. As a guide on these trails, one did not sleep soundly when lion were around, and the idea of a problem in the night after our rhino experience did not allow me that luxury of deep sleep.

After breakfast of cereal and tea, we dropped our packs near the game trail and set off to scan the lower hills for game. I loved to sit on the rocks right on the crest of the hill and scan the foothills, lakeshore, and treelines for any movement. Frequently, rhino, buffalo, or other game would be spotted, feeding quietly and the vantage point of the hilltop was acutely realised. It was very rewarding, and often saved me walking into rhino and other game coming up the hill, for I too used the game trails created by generations of wildlife moving up and down the hills.

Eventually, we moved off and started the long descent to the lakeshore for the night. It was surprising how far from the lake hippo would forage when grass was scarce, and I often found their spoor and dung scattered over the trails way up in the hills. It was about four o'clock when we finally started to hit the flatter ground, and the woodland opened up due to the soil erosion and the topography changed. We walked past a few thickets, and I spotted the tawny bodies of sleeping lions, literally fifteen metres away. Not breaking my stride, I grabbed Anne's arm and told Michael, 'Lions……. keep walking!' The lions grunted and most ran off, but two young males growled and made a short rush at us. I shouted and waved my hat at them. They backed off, growling and snarling their displeasure and followed their siblings, reluctantly, stopping to watch us walk on. Michael and Ann were mute with surprise and fright. 'Why didn't they charge us?' she asked eventually, 'They were SO CLOSE!'

'Well, the two young boys did, but it's best to just keep going sometimes,' I answered. 'It takes the wind out of their sails,' I smiled at her. She shook her neat, short-cropped head.

I decided that we should walk further than I had previously intended, as their behaviour had bothered me. I explained that I had felt we should cover a good distance from the lions before bedding down for the night. They agreed, and so we pushed quite hard until about five o'clock.

I found a good site for the night. A sheer cliff on one side of about twelve feet, next to a river bed, and a large Umbrella thorn tree that elephants had pushed over . . . this covered the three sides. I cut and pulled more thorn branches in to effectively seal the third side of the triangle. I felt more secure about the site, and we were only about ten yards from the edge of the lake. Michael had set up his hammock, Anne had a secure patch under the big tree itself, and I was on the edge. We had dinner, coffee, and were feeling good about the trip.

Anne offered to accompany me to wash the dishes down at the waters' edge, and so off we went, leaving Michael in his hammock. My rifle was on my bed.

We had just finished the few dishes, and Anne was chatting when I thought I heard a noise up at the camp. I shushed her and grabbed her hand to stop her talking. She looked surprised. 'Michael', I shouted. No answer. I had a bad premonition. Scooping up a fist-sized stone, my torch, and the plates, I grabbed Anne, and we rushed back up the slope towards the camp, calling Michael's name. Silence. As we reached the lip, Michael's calm voice came out of the darkness. 'Gavin, there's a lion right next to me. He's just tried to get in.'

I flashed the torch and there, a scant few yards off was crouched a young two-year-old lion, glaring at me. I threw the stone hard and with all my strength. It hit him hard high on his shoulder, and he sprang into the air with a loud snarl. Whirling around, I picked up my rifle and checked the load. I had put soft-nose rounds in the magazine for just this situation. I chambered a round and locked the safety on. The lion had disappeared, but I wasn't taking any chances. 'Michael, are you OK?' I flashed the torch on him, and he was lying with his arms behind his head, a week's growth on his chin, and a lazy smile on his face. 'That lion was so close I smelt his breath. He had a go at me through the thorns and couldn't get through,' he stated slowly . . . so calm. 'Bloody amazing,' I thought.

I placed Anne under her bush and checked my defences. We could not have a fire as it was the dry season and my torch was the only light we had. Suddenly, lion roars started from the bush beyond us. They reverberated right through us all. He was facing us and roaring his displeasure at our presence. I could see we were in for a sleepless night . . . again.

Placing my rifle close at hand, I collected a pile of stones that I could use. Out in the river bed, about fifty yards away, about six pairs of glassy green eyes reflected the pathetic light from my torch.

The rest of the pride . . . now, *that* was trouble if they decided to come all at once. I would be forced to shoot a couple at least, the last resort, but I would do it. Lions are lions and we weren't short of lions in the wild.

I decided to make a fire. Going out and collecting what wood I could, knowing there was a very angry lion prowling around was an interesting experience, and I soon had a good pile of wood that I knew would last several hours at least. Then out of nowhere, the wind came up. So typical of the hot months when the ground temperatures of 44 °C would generate incredible high winds.

This meant I wasn't going to be able to hear what was sneaking around the camp.

I double-checked our thorn barrier and raised it a little. That lion could easily have leapt over the barrier, grabbed Michael, and got out again. All the time, his roars echoed about the hills and over the lake. Once the fire was going, I instructed Anne to keep it well fed. Amazing how a false confidence is generated once we can see. I collected more firewood and got stung by a scorpion in the process . . . things were getting interesting.

We sat and talked. I tried to keep it light-hearted, and they were both so good and relaxed. 'Michael, you were amazing,' I said. 'Most people would have died of fright, and you Anne, have been *so* helpful. Thank you both.' They were so relaxed. 'Gavin, you have it under control. We're not concerned. If you had ever panicked, it would have shown by now, and we have faith in you. Don't worry. Let's make some tea.' So we spent the night. The wind blew sparks all over us and scattered orange darts through the thorns as well. It was a surreal few hours . . . a lion roaring, wind howling hot wind, and the fire burning horizontally, while we tried to brew never-ending mugs of tea.

Twice that lion came up close, and twice I pelted him with stones and even pursued him into the darkness. The wind became a real nuisance, and I was glad that there was no grass to catch fire. Lions *and* a bushfire, I couldn't get away with.

That lion roared at us until three o'clock in the morning, before settling down just out of torch range, growling whenever one of us stood up and moved around. At five in the morning, he moved off, following the rest who had left sometime around midnight.

The morning light was most welcome, and as soon as it was light enough, we set off to see what the spoor was going to reveal. The group of six had never moved closer than when I had first spotted them. The male, on the other hand, had paced around the whole area, and his spoor, clear and proud, was everywhere. I found three places where he had lain down just out of the range of the firelight, his paws tucked under him facing us. The wind had erased most of his spoor, but this was evidence enough that he had evil intent.

Our boat arrived at eight thirty, and we embarked with a story to tell.

I conducted trails in the Matusadona for several years and never had a problem with lions even though I had lions walk right through my camp and next to it on several occasions. This particular young male was of a different genre, and I am glad to say I never met him again.

SPRINGS AND THINGS

During the early post-independence years, the BMATT (British Military Advisory Training Team) personnel who were stationed in Zimbabwe had a fine time traveling and seeing the country. I was very fortunate in meeting a number of fine men from the officer cadre, and, eventually, managed to persuade a few of them to 'do' a wilderness trail with me. One such adventure I recall with considerable humour.

We were a group of seven and had chosen to walk in mid-October when the ambient temperatures were around 40C. Humidity was almost zero, and the dry heat sucked the moisture out of anyone walking anywhere in the Zambezi Valley. The impala would be in the shade by nine o'clock in the morning. We walked about eight kilometres on that first afternoon and based up on the high bank of a river bed, out of reach of any flash flood waters. Most of the men carried three or even four one-litre water bottles, which I had scoffed at as it seemed a little over the top, in view of the fact that there was water available from time to time.

That night we were exceptionally thirsty, except those that had kept their four bottles. At midnight, a dry electric storm had woken us with a huge din and electric-blue lightning flared across the sky. The lip of the escarpment was lit up with a rolling display of the most incredible intensity and the blooming cumulonimbus clouds were filled with light as well. It was quite breath taking, even though we were thirsty . . . some of us anyway.

The men immediately erected water traps with their bivvies, and positioned their water bottles to catch the anticipated deluge. We waited and watched . . . and waited. Not a drop fell, and we had a sleepless night to boot. Early the next morning, tea was for 'sale' for some . . . all in good-natured fun. We set off, with me assuring everybody that not far up the way was a lovely spring, with fresh, clear water.

Cheered by this promise, we struck camp and were soon on the trail heading south to the base of the hills. In a short time, we came upon some wet muddy footprints of a bull elephant. 'There we go,' I said cheerfully, there's water around somewhere. We carried on, the men talking quietly amongst themselves as we did so.

On trail, it generally takes a few days for a routine to develop. First, its packing the pack with most used items at the top, then others in the middle, and of course, bedding as well. Some packs had separate compartments for sleeping bags and mosquito nets, which obviated the need to unpack everything every night before bedtime. Generally, setting up camp was carried out in daylight as was cooking the evening meal. It just made life easier, and it ensured minimum movement after dark as accidents with scorpions, snakes, and predators were more likely to happen in the dark period.

We carried on for a few kilometres, seeing an old bull elephant walking through the bush, some buffalo and even two fabulous kudu bulls browsing along a gulley. The escarpment edge loomed ahead, and I found very fresh rhino spoor heading away from us again. 'OK, you guys, there's a rhino around here somewhere. Keep your eyes peeled for something large, brown and wet, with two points on one end.' My attempt at humour was met with silence. I knew where that rhino had just come from. Oh dear . . . , my spring.

A few minutes later, we arrived at the base of the hill. I climbed a small tree to check that we weren't interrupting any large animal having its bath.

There was a large roundish pool of mud, with a few elephant turds plonked along the edge, like giant vegetarian ice-cream scoops. To complete the picture, the pool was a smooth, chocolate brown pudding, poured perfectly into a shallow basin. I looked at it and smiled at the assembled company. 'Here we are then, fresh water in a jiffy. Thank goodness!' Their faces were a study in abject disbelief and shock. 'That's the spring?' Just enough horror to balance the disbelief. I answered, 'Yup, that's my spring, and look the water still coming through. Fantastic.' I slipped my pack off, and took my trusty, orange, plastic plate out of my pack. Unscrewing the lid from my water bottle, I knelt next to the pool of chocolate, and waited. The men paused a moment and wandered off to a shady tree, and sat down in a disconsolate group, muttering. 'Why don't you lot make some tea. I'll bring you some fresh water in a few minutes,' I called out to them.

I was waiting for the cool, clear water to force its way to the top, which it did, creating a clean layer of water. It was into this that I slipped my plate, filling it. I carefully filled my water bottle, and took it over to the men, offered it to them to use for tea. One of them, a colonel took it gingerly and opened the lid. 'Amazing,' he smiled. 'What did you do?' . . . 'Waited for clean water, that's all,' I returned the smile.

I held out my hands for their water bottles which they offered hesitantly . . . just some of them. I returned to my task, and within half an hour had filled them all. They checked them, and thanked me. One offered me some tea in his mug. 'You know, Gavin, our version of a clear water spring, is different to yours'.

That spring never let me down in all the years I wandered about the mountains and bush there. That's why the rhino knew it was there.

Later on in the same walk, I again was looking for water, and took some of the men to some rocks, and asked them to look for water. 'Here,' they asked. I nodded. 'What do you see?' They were puzzled. Waiting for them to answer, 'Watch for the insects and birds as they need water all the time.' A steady stream of bees flew unseen by the men, to a clump of rocks in the cliff. I took out my plate again, and with my arm at full stretch into a crack in the rock face collected a plateful of water. They were amazed, and again we filled our bottles from the earth. Blue waxbills and bulbuls ventured to the foot of the rocks when we had moved away, and sipped the moisture with delicate bills, drop by drop.

These BMATT officers were some of the finest calibre men I have ever met, and it was a great privilege to be among them for those few short years.

BIG SNAKES AND LITTLE SNAKES

'Stretch' A. J. Ferreira and I have known each other for over forty years. His lanky frame and red beard are one of the best sights I know of when I'm feeling down or just looking for a soul mate in the Zambezi Valley. Stretch and I have done many trails together, and one small incident comes to mind, also in the Matusadona.

Like many people, Stretch is not fond of snakes, and although he will not go out of his way to kill one, he doesn't like them at all. He was on a wilderness trail with some BMATT fellows and me in the Matusadona. We had made camp in a patch of long grass, not my first choice, but we had been caught out late, and it was quite comfortable having a grassy mattress for a change, not just hard ground as normal. We had all been asleep for an hour or so, and it was around nine or ten o'clock at night. I was sleeping on my stomach when I felt the cool slide of a small snake over my bare legs. I was alert in an instant and lay absolutely still, trying to figure out how big, how fat, and how far up it had slid against me. What might it be? I lay there for a while longer and, eventually, called to Stretch, who was sleeping a short distance away from me. 'Stretch, I've got a snake in my bed. Get a torch and see what it is before I move, please.' There was absolute silence.

'What?' His lanky frame raised itself from the folds of his net, looking ghost-like in the pale starlight. 'I've got a sna . . .'

'I heard, I heard . . . I *don't* want to see this, damn it.'

I waited patiently as he grumbled and mumbled his way cautiously over to my bed. The torch flashed through my net. I peered over my shoulder and saw the snake. 'It's OK. It's just a very large centipede eater,' I stated with relief. It could have been a young spitting cobra as they are nocturnal, and a young agile cobra in bed would have been tricky for me to deal with.

The others did not stir, so I gently caught it, examined it in the light, and slipped it out of my net into the grass. 'Thanks, Stretch.'

He didn't answer me, just ambled back to bed, shuffling and muttering. I was about to go to sleep again, when Stretch exploded, 'Damn it, Ford. *Why* did you have to show me that snake?' He shuffled and fidgeted for much of the night after that. He's never forgotten that I owe him at least one good night's rest.

Snakes were never a problem on my trails, and we saw a good number of these maligned creatures.

On another trip, with a group of businessmen from Harare who were on a hiking experience with me, we had just enjoyed a lunch break in some dense mopane scrub, and were having a post lunch nap. We all dispersed to various patches within a short distance of each other and after unrolling sleeping bags or groundsheets, went to sleep. I stayed awake for a short while, and then drifted off into my customary fifteen-minute power-nap.

I awoke and checked my watch. Time to move. I stood up and dusted myself off, checked my pack, rifle, and hat, and moved my pack to a central point before going to wake everybody up.

One of my walkers in particular was fast asleep, with his head half under the leafy young branches of a mopane bush, and what he didn't know was that he was sharing the bush with something as relaxed as he was. There was a ten-foot African python lying curled up on the other side of his bush. I knew there was not any real danger to my guest, so I didn't wake him up right then but quietly summoned the others first to see our slumbering friend and his unusual bed mate. In fact, we took a photo. The python watched us with a glassy stare, its softly flickering tongue picking up our scent as we slowly moved about it taking photos of the scene. It was a fairly large snake, and I was amazed that Mike had not seen it when he had chosen this spot to lie down.

I woke my walker and pulled him slowly up with an extended arm, in a friendly gesture. As he sat up, he realised he was the centre of attention and grinned good-naturedly at his slothfulness . . . until the others gestured to the back of the bush. He peered backwards, and, with a loud yell, sprang forward from a sitting position on to his feet, completely ruining the calm of the moment. 'Relax, Mike,' I tried to calm him down. 'The snake's been there all along. He's very happy being your mate, now stop fussing.' We quickly gathered our packs and moved out. The python was still there, quietly waiting with reptilian patience for its own time to move out.

Snakes always feature as a part of any discussion about the bush, and invariably somebody knows somebody who was nearly bitten or was chased or had some narrow escape from a slavering reptile way over the official record size. Black mambas generally feature prominently in any bushlore, and so I will add two of my own stories to the legends that abound about this notorious and very interesting snake. These stories are true.

The Matusadona National Park is a well-known park in Zimbabwe, and I was privileged to spend about thirteen years of my career walking it from all corners of its boundaries. During these walks I saw a number of these snakes, and only a handful of times did I feel personally threatened. I have seen mambas many times in my travels, but these occasions were particularly memorable as they were my first encounters with a mamba.

MAMBA MEMORIES

I need to explain to some readers who may not appreciate the danger that a mamba bite presents. Mamba bites are normally very strong, incredibly quick, and neurotoxic in effect. In short, the victim suffers shortness of breath and paralysis, and then ceases to breath and then naturally dies. Most unattended deaths occur within an hour or two. *Not* every bite is deadly, and several people have survived the bite, *but* because they received qualified medical assistance within a short period after the bite. A mamba bite, deep in the bush, is not likely to have a happy ending.

I was on a morning walk along the Kaingwe River, with four middle aged guests who were gratifyingly interested in everything that I drew their attention to. We had spent a very satisfying few hours talking about the bush, trees, spoor, followed an elephant bull as he went about his business for a while, and were talking about termites. I was walking through an area badly criss-crossed by trees felled by elephants. These mopane boughs last for years without being eaten by termites, and I was about to mention this when I saw a fairly large black mamba basking on one of these, which was adjacent to a termite mound. We were about ten metres from the snake, and it was a simultaneous sighting as there was no cover except a few stumps. I stopped talking and stood still. 'Stand still, everybody. There's a black mamba.'

There was a shuffling behind me as the party gathered behind me to see this new item of interest . . . 'Stand absolutely still, please,' I said again, swiftly unslinging my rifle and cocking it, holding it at the ready, barrel at waist height in front of me. The snake raised itself off the tree trunk, and watched us nervously, its beady black eyes shiny in the morning sun. I waited. Still. The snake watched us and then slowly slid forward along its trunk towards me. It was about five metres away and stopped watching me intently. It was a moment of awe and acute concern. Here was one of the world's most deadly snakes, and it was right there in front of me.

We stared at each other for a few moments. I tried speaking without moving my mouth. 'The snake is just studying us, seeing if we are a threat. DO NOT MOVE.' I had an itch on my cheek. I was wondering if I should shoot it if it decided to move any closer, so I inched the end of my rifle towards it, judging the angle at this close distance. I hoped that the muzzle blast alone would disorient it, even if I actually missed it, giving me time to reload and finish it at point-blank range. The snake then suddenly slid to the ground and reared up, its mouth half open and spread a slight hood. The inside of its mouth was a soft, moist pit of dark olive, from whence the mamba derives its name. The upper body was tense as a bow, and I realised that there had been movement behind me.

I heard a faint, 'Oh my goodness, I'm so scared . . . oh.' It was one of my female guests, a delightful English woman who was a real nature-lover. I braced myself for the shock of the recoil as I knew this was my limit. Strangely enough, I felt no fear of the snake, only a huge admiration as it was truly a beautiful animal standing tall and fearless against us. The top of its head must have been about three and half feet off the ground. 'KEEP STILL', I lisped as loud as I dared. I was reluctant to shoot it, but I had no choice. I gripped the rifle tightly, getting ready to fire. After a few minutes the snake backed off. It slid backwards and away from us, its lowered head tilted to one side, watching us intently, its long olive grey body reshaping itself as it distanced itself from us. I gulped involuntarily . . . my itch suddenly returned, maddeningly worse. I dared not move. A fly landed on my nose, sipping the sweat. I tried to blow it off and it moved.

Silence. The snake continued to move diagonally away from us, slowly now and then stopped. It was a good fifteen metres away off, and heading away from us to the edge of the termite mound. I spoke loudly, 'Now, *slowly* back away, please, starting with the back person. Do it now. Go!' I heard soft noises and scrunches of gravel. I was watching the snake very carefully for any sign of a return. 'Just keep moving away from the snake. Do not stop to look, please.' The shuffly noises moved away, and I risked a glance backwards. I started to move *very* slowly, backwards, keeping an open line between myself and the snake so that I could see it all the time. We kept moving until I deemed it safe to stop briefly well away from the termite mound, and then I moved the group together, after checking if everybody was OK.

Eventually, we gathered under some shade and could relax. They all had different perspectives on it. 'Was it going to bite us?'

'Is it that dangerous?'

'I was terrified out of my wits, and thought I was going to embarrass myself. Talking of which, I need a loo stop urgently.'

We sat and chatted about this amazing experience, and I had to go over it several times for them. They were enthralled, even though two of them sneakingly admitted that they didn't like snakes, but *this one* had really been impressive. My little English lady said in shocked tones, 'I never realised they were so big and fierce . . . He was looking straight at me.'

She had put on her glasses to see better.

What a morning that was!

In retrospect, many will say I should have shot the snake when it reared up so close to us. I may or may not have been successful in killing it. I took the chance as the snake was hesitant, and I 'read' that, and took a few moments before shooting. Those few moments made the difference for my guests between a traumatic and negative experience (and holiday), and something incredible they will remember for the rest of their lives . . . *and* I saved the snake's life too.

The next mamba story is equally interesting, and I have chosen an incident that occurred in Botswana. I was on a short morning walk in the Okavango Delta, with some travel agents, who were about to depart for another camp. They had wanted to walk as it was a lovely morning, and I always try and make people aware of how special it is to be on the ground and at 'eye level' with what's going on in the bush. There were four of them, and one of them was rather large and ungainly, with an unfortunate propensity for finding and falling in every small depression or springhare burrow within ten feet of her. Some folks are just like that.

I had chosen an easy open area to traverse as we were short of time, and I wanted them to have a something positive to talk about. The grassland was part of the annual flood area, but as the flood was still months away, there were still items of interest, to stop and to examine. Of course, there was a chance elephants would walk out of the woodland at any point or giraffes would emerge to feed along the fringe of the acacia woodlands too. The resident impala bounced away to watch us from a distance. The Burchell's starlings were noisy and a small flight of cattle egrets passed over us, heading up between the trees of the watercourse, looking for a herd of buffalo or a large game to settle amongst and feed. The woodland birds are always fun to identify, and their different calls make it all the more interesting for visitors.

We had reached a termite mound that had a skirt of young ivory palms and thorn bushes growing around it. Two tall palms reached for the sky on the one side, and it was these that I wanted to stop at and talk about – palm swifts, palm nuts, and the trees' use generally. As we moved around the one side of the mound, I stepped into a large depression that the elephants had excavated with their broad feet in search for roots. Above me was a very dense low thorn bush, projecting about three feet above my head that the giraffe had cropped to a neat rounded top. I stopped and turned, waiting for my happy walkers to join me. As they did so, the 'larger' walker tripped, stumbled, and recovered herself, with a yelp. I managed to catch her and helped her to steady herself. At that moment, there was a thrashing around in the thorn bush right above me and the group.

In a split second, I realised it was a large snake and had unslung my rifle and cocked it, pointing the barrel at the noise. A huge black mamba emerged from the bush, literally two feet from the barrel. It had been dozing in the morning sun when we had disturbed it.

The snake came out and realised it could not reverse due to the thorns. So it came out in a huge loop, head tilted to one side as it passed overhead, watching us. It then went straight back into the bush followed by all ten feet plus of its thickened and charcoal-brown snake body. It hardly made a sound. I gazed at it in wonder and in silence, too amazed to speak. As the last part fed into the bush, I told the women what it was. 'Wasn't that incredible!' I was beside myself with awe. 'That is one of the biggest mambas I have ever seen, and certainly that's the closest you ever want to get to one.' I was really pleased. The women were not really impressed, but agreed that it was something to remember. They wanted to see elephants and lions.

The only feedback I received from that particular activity was that I had walked them too hard and the ground was terribly uneven. You can only please some people. Dear, oh dear!

CANOEING THE ZAMBEZI

In the mid-1980s, canoeing the Zambezi became one of the most popular tourist activities for anybody visiting southern Africa, particularly, Zimbabwe. Canoeing companies employed young men who had all the attributes necessary to run a trip safely and 'professionally'. This included a great sense of fun and adventure, a well-developed sense of responsibility, the ability to get on well with and manage people from all walks of life and various cultures. Most of all they had to be resourceful. As there were no benchmark principles to go by, the industry essentially created its' own rules. And so after a couple of years of operating (and a steep and exciting collective learning curve, which ultimately was the best way for the industry to evolve), it took a near-fatal incident with a lion and an extremely courageous young canoe guide, named Troy Williamson, before national parks became aware that in fact, canoe guides needed some form of training and legal qualification to satisfy the insurance system in case of liability claims.

As the only members of the Zimbabwe Professional Hunters and Guides Association (ZPHGA) with any experience in this field, John Stevens, Justin Seymour Smith, and I were tasked with interviewing candidates and conducting canoeing proficiency tests, which we did under the able chairmanship of Bruce Austin, the then chairman of the association.

John had been one of the original shareholders of Canoeing Safaris, along with Eddie Rous, who had first started the canoeing business.

This we did, and through interviewing candidates, all of whom had been canoeing the river for some time by then, and by conducting proficiency tests (with a member of national parks with us) on the river over several days we were able to recommend to parks, as the licensing authority, individuals for canoe guides licenses. As there was no provision in the Wildlife Act (1974) for this type of license, a 'River Guide Authority' was issued instead. It holds to this day.

Several canoeing companies had been formed, and the operators and national parks (as the licensing authority) had to formulate a system whereby the quality of the experience was not compromised by the sudden huge demand for this activity; such was its popularity. By dividing the river downstream from Kariba wall to Kanyemba into three sections and ensuring that departures did not overlap, on each section, canoeists never saw another canoe safari during their trip. Litter was scrupulously collected and guides were taught to remember to remove marks of the canoes on the beaches when they landed. Going to the toilet was a simple matter of digging a small hole with a hoe or a shovel, a roll of toilet paper, and some matches to burn the paper!

All other litter was 'bagged' to be removed to Kariba or the 'pull-out point'.

It was the most wonderful adventure for visitors to canoe this river, and the Zambezi touched everybody who ventured on its waters.

Naturally, there was provision for any Zimbabwean to also book for a 'self-guided' canoe trip, and these launch days were hotly contested. The experience was not confined to operators, and the system worked very well.

The stories of what happened on these safaris that now span nearly twenty-eight years are legendary and will be written about elsewhere. I humbly submit some of my own experiences for fun.

There was a time when I used to do freelance trips for a very good friend of mine, Andrew 'Stretch' Ferreira, who still owns and runs Goliath Safaris. His trips were normally busy and one never knew what sort of persons one was going to have to keep company with and get down the river.

One particular trip comes to mind, when I was doing a trip for Goliath Safaris from Kariba to Mana Pools. The vehicle had collected the clients from the Bronte Hotel, in Harare, as usual and had driven up to Kariba on the same morning. I was already in Kariba and waiting at the top of the gorge. Fani, the driver, eventually arrived and after introducing myself and getting all of the gear together we set off down to the river, a walk of about two kilometres over a rough, narrow, stony path through the hills and, eventually, the river. It was always a little test of the mettle of the clients as it was invariably hot, steep, and difficult, and we were always carrying some item of equipment or personal gear. The porters were paid to carry the canoes and camping gear, which they appeared to do with relative ease, having done it for years.

On arrival at the river side, I gathered my guests and gave them a briefing on the procedures for the next few days. I allocated them canoes, chose partners for them, told them how to stow their kit safely, and asked them all to make sure that they had all been to the toilet (the 'loo') before we started. Then I told them to reassemble for the 'Safety Briefing'.

They were a mixed crew for certain – two young American women, travelling together and 'involved', a Swede, a Belgian, two Greek South Africans, businessmen on a personal journey, and two young men from the UK. I sat them down in the shade and began my introduction to the river, giving some of its history and, of course, the dangerous aspects of the river . . . the sun, stumps, hippo, and crocodiles. This was the first reaction I had got from the crew. The Belgian sat up suddenly, his eyes wide in alarm. 'Zere are crocodiles in here and Zippos? But why did not anybody tell me about zees?'

I was shocked . . . and frowned at this unexpected news in Franco English.

'Well, I'm sure you were told in Harare when Sarah gave you your preliminary briefing yesterday.'

I was being patient.

'*No*, no . . .' His eyes wide with surprise and panic.

'Well, I'm afraid I will have to ask you then if you wish to continue with the safari, as we all are, unless anybody else has any objections to crocodiles and to hippos in the Zambezi.' I looked around at the group. The South Africans were laughing quietly to themselves in disbelief. 'Hey, Boet, don't worry. There's enough choice here, and Carel here is much fatter than you.' They laughed good-naturedly, their gold chains nestling in their dense chest hair.

'Well, what choice do I have,' he asked. 'Do I walk back up the hill on my own to the car and wait zumwhere for you to finish the trip?' Fani had walked down with us just in case there were any last-minute changes, such as this, and he would have walked the client out. However, I preferred to try and smooth it all over as canoeing is such a wonderful way to see the river.

'You definitely would have been told. Who was there for the briefing yesterday afternoon?' I asked, looking around. Three of the group raised their hands.

'Was he there?'

They nodded. 'But I was very tired,' he interjected. 'I slept a little.' He shrugged.

'Is it zafe? Don't crocodiles eat people?'

I told him that it was safe as long as one obeyed the rules and didn't swim or dangle body parts like arms and legs in the water. He looked nonplussed, shrugged, and then smiled.

'OK, I go,' he said agreeably.

'Ozzerwise, you wouldn't be in business, no?' I smiled back at him, thanked him for being sensible, and agreed with him. Everybody nodded and we carried on. 'This is the *front* of the canoe, and this is the back. The person at the back is responsible for steering the canoe *and* paddling too. The person in front listens to instructions that I will shout back to you all and looks out for obstacles in the river . . . , which he will pass on to the fellow behind him.' I continued, 'This is how you hold a paddle . . . etc . . .'

After my briefing, which included a simple demonstration on 'How to paddle a canoe', we embarked on our trip. I told them to stay in the calm water area and practice some of the strokes I had described to them. Immediately, chatter and splashes engulfed the launch bay. The staff and porters watched in amazement and complete astonishment at the ease with which these white foreigners turned a simple task into a 'life or death' mission. Their white teeth gleamed behind their hands as they watched. (It's very impolite to laugh at someone you don't know.) I watched too, in amusement as simple instructions became a fraught exercise. I was used to this, but it still amazed me. 'Crickey, and I'm supposed to get these people down the Zambezi safely and alive. Look out hippos, here we come,' I thought to myself.

I gathered my motley crew. 'All right, you lot. Listen in! No teaspoon paddlers here. OK. Your paddles must go deep, a full blade. Make sure the bloody blade is facing right way too or it will be hopeless. Don't forget, you can only steer the canoe *if* you are going faster than the current, *or* you are moving the water faster than the canoe. *If* . . . you are paddling harder than the slow water. Comprende? Remember, you paddle a backstroke to brake. Either left side or right side.' I recited the instructions again and made them all carry out these simple manoeuvres until I thought they had made progress. I heard a soft comment, 'You mean the paddles got a front and a back?' Curiosity and wonder in the voice . . . Odi.

'Down here a short way is a *big rock*, half submerged on the right-hand side. *It* will cause you a problem if you go anywhere near it, so follow me to the left side of the middle of the river. Is that clear? There is an obstacle on the left, so we cannot go on the *Zambian* side, OK?' Nearly everyone nodded. 'Carel, Odi?'. The two Greeks. They smiled, and I had an uneasy feeling about them. 'They will get it soon enough,' I thought and lead the way out into the main current. I let the canoe drift, paddling slowly to allow everybody to fall into line behind me.

The black rocky cliffs are shear and high, over a thousand feet as you traverse the gorge. I pointed out the high watermark, where the floods used to reach before the barrier of the dam wall was erected. 'In 1958, the flood waters rose fifty feet overnight and destroyed the cofferdams. Those floods were repeated the following season too. Can you imagine?' I asked to no one in particular . . . just enjoying being on the river again. I constantly monitored my flotilla during the first hour as this was a fraught time. We had passed 'Floating Rock' as we called it, without casualties . . . all in good order. Except for Carel and Odi, who had passed it facing backwards. These two had earned an early distinction. They talked. A constant flow of verbiage issued forth, and with it a complete lack of skill in understanding the subtle nuances of the canoe's 'needs' if it was to follow the faithful line behind me.

Their canoe would take the initiative and head off across the river, and they would be oblivious to the fact that they were heading for a rock or the cliff face, all the while maintaining a constant flow of talk. I had canoed this river many times, and it was a major concern getting everybody down it safely, and these two were not going to allow me to relax.

They had careened off the walls of the gorge, breaking the nose-ring off the boat . . . in fact, pushing it into the body of the canoe. Oblivious to this it seemed, and amid much loud profanity, funny but fraught, they had then 'cartwheeled' downriver with the current pushing them despite all their splashing and paddling forwards and backwards, quite often at the same time in opposite directions. I had laughed and laughed, turning the incident into a joke and easing the tension I felt from the other canoeists. The Swede, Gotty, was very solemn, whilst Bernhardt had eventually loosened up sufficiently to make several remarks in his very Germanic accent, which, of course, made it all the funnier. The young Brits were very quiet and hardly made any contribution to the general chatter, just an occasional comment, their eyes shining with excitement. We had pause to examine the plaque to Steve Edwards's father high up on a facing rock. Steve and his friend had paddled the Zambezi from above the lake in the late 1960s. That was another saga.

The two American women were quite competent in a canoe. After they had changed seats and paddled for a while, they changed back again, deciding that they both were equal to the task of paddling (from the stern), steering and just providing paddle power. Their names were Mary-Jane (preferred Mary) and Kate. They just paddled and followed instructions and got along fine, chatting quietly to themselves and asking me questions about the river whenever they were alongside. Peter and Mark were the two English boys, both on gap years away from the 'north country', and their accents ear-marked them for a few wise cracks from The Greeks.

I had made a few stops during this first half-day paddling to rest everybody and let them enjoy this magnificent setting. The folding pattern in the rocks were so clearly apparent illustrating the ancient forces that had moulded the hills towering over us. Once we had seen the silhouette of an elephant on the Zambian bank, right at the edge of the cliff, and I had pulled the canoes over to the side to watch it for a moment. 'I didn't know elephants could climb' had been a remark from somebody. Without seeing who it was I had answered, 'They can go most places a man can go unaided . . . except up sheer cliffs. The elephant has walked along the top of the mountain ridge.' There was a moment's silence whilst everybody digested this . . . 'You mean there's a mountain on the other side of this cliff?'.....a question from some bright spark.

'Sure thing'.

I smiled at my canoeists. 'There's a whole line of mountains.'

Towards the afternoon, we approached the mouth of the gorge at Nyamumba, where we would be overnight on the huge sandy island at the bend of the river. I motioned everybody to come alongside, and we rafted for a short distance . . . everybody except Odi and Carel who paused in their 'labours' to hear what I said, 'OK, listen in. There is a herd of hippo on the right-hand side of the island, and the current is strong too. If you go too wide, you will be taken straight over the hippo, which normally are on the bend.' I paused to let this information sink in, looking straight at Carel and Odi.

'OK, guys, so take it slow, and we will hug the inside of the island because this is where we are going to camp tonight on the Zimbabwean side of the island. We will go down the inside of the island slowly and then pull-out about halfway down.' I smiled at everybody to reassure them that all would be well. Well, they were a lot more competent than they had been five hours previously, and it wasn't that hard.

We drifted for a short while and then I broke the 'raft' up and took the lead, the canoes straggling out behind me . . . except for Carl and Odi. Their canoe took a new course, straight for the Zambian bank, again. 'Slowly, *slowly*,' I shouted, wincing as the nose of their craft hit the rocks . . . There was an awful lot of instructions being given and counter-given. They were starting to spin down the river again. I already knew what was going to happen unless I intervened. I back paddled and then stroked hard to intercept them as they broke free of the gorge. The sudden change to open flatland here was sudden and a welcome change. There was a problem with the Greek's canoe. The nose-ring had been pushed into the fibreglass body at the seam, so I tried to get Odi to push it back using the back of his paddle. It splintered unhelpfully, and so I came alongside and told him to hook his leg over my canoe's side whilst they both paddled on the other. Easy with their canoe now 'attached' to mine, we paddled slowly towards the tip of the island, slowly feeling the current push us faster and faster. Gravel scrunched underneath us as we skimmed the bottom. The water was always clear here where the current divided at the tip of the island.

The other canoes had successfully negotiated the course and were ahead of us, heading towards the middle of the island and drifting slowly in an unhurried manner, out of the push of the current. I whistled and waved my arm towards the bank. 'Pull in on the corner'. The girls and the two English boys waved and eased their canoe nose into the bank, and the other canoe followed. They climbed out, waiting for us. They were a little short of our stop, so I waited until we were closer before I told them where we were to stop. There were no stumps or landmarks in those days, just a sandy beach, but the current had created a slight shelf, and it was easier and safer there. (the whole island has changed dramatically in the intervening years as floods have remoulded the sand and trees have grown there now.) We were ahead of the other canoes, and they quickly climbed back in and started off behind us.

The Greeks had not stopped talking once during this whole interlude, and I had told them when to paddle and warned them what to do. We approached the stop-point, moving faster than I intended. 'OK, boys, paddle on the right. Hard!' I wanted to swing the canoes hard round. It should have been simple and controlled. I braked gently to facilitate the turn. Odi's leg came up, and he fell over in his seat. He dropped his paddle. My canoe hit the sand. Their canoe, travelling faster than mine also hit the sand, but harder and the back spun around. Odi sat up, shouting at Carel. 'Paddle hard', he bellowed, now also paddling with his hands like a frantic windmill. His paddle was nowhere to be seen. (It was next to the hull) Carel backpaddled and then realising his error, tried to change sides and paddle forwards. Odi's frantic efforts were creating a veritable waterfall, soaking Carel completely. Fear of the hippo was now firmly in their minds, kinship and history long forgotten. The canoe was eagerly snatched up by the current and started to spin backwards going faster and faster. They were by now screaming at each other. Odi's paddle bobbed merrily in the current a couple of metres from me.

I couldn't believe it. One moment it had all been calm and controlled, and now there was a potential disaster unravelling before my eyes. Carel had stopped paddling, and Odi was half turned in his seat, abusing his friend. The other two canoes had pulled in next to me and were watching, round eyed. 'Stay here and pull your canoes out. This is the camp. I'll be back now,' I shouted.

'Mary, jump into my canoe, please. Just remove the bags there.' Grasping the urgency of it all, she threw everything out of the front seat, jumped in, and the others pushed us off. The other canoe of the Greeks was now spinning languidly heading straight for the far corner where the pink and brown heads of the Nyamumba hippo pod stared in menacing expectation. The two men franticly paddling with their hands and the one paddle. The current was swift here, and I made good speed with Mary pulling well. 'We won't catch them before the hippo, but we will be ready on the other side to the corner there.'

'The current is really swift, and there's always crocs there as well.' She turned and looked at me, 'You're joking?' I shook my head, she just turned back and sat for a moment, paddle over her knees. 'Paddle, girl, we need to be there quickly,' I injected urgency into my voice. She paddled.

The Greeks went straight over the hippo. The hippo had watched with disbelief as the canoe, suddenly picked up a little speed and headed straight for them. At the last minute, several had blown sprays of water into the air and dived for the bottom of the river, only a few metres down. The nose of the Greek's canoe had cut through the surface swirls, and I had waited for something to happen. I glanced at the bend, two big crocodiles were ponderously waddling down to the water's edge, before sliding in. I looked back, nothing had happened . . . I shouted to them to head for the bank . . . why, I don't really know, but the canoe responded. The prow of the canoe almost ramped the steep beach and successfully grounded itself, flinging both occupants forward. Both still abusing each other. Mary and I turned against the river, pulling hard, and downstream of the hippo. Several had run underneath us, their big brown bodies clearly seen as they trundled away in clouds of river sand off the bottom. Mary had been silent. 'Damn, this girl was good,' I thought to myself. We collected the lost paddle.

We were right up against the edge of the bank and slowly moved against the current. 'OK, Mary, can you climb out and hold the canoe for me, please?'

She climbed out and steadied the boat. I climbed out, and we walked slowly up to the Greeks. They were *still* abusing each other, faces flushed and swarthy with five o'clock shadow.

They paused as we stopped. 'OK, guys. Calm down. Calm down, for Pete's sake!' I soothed, hoping to placate them.

'You're OK, and the hippos are gone for now. Let's go.'

'Let's go . . . That's all you say?'

Odi glared at me.

'Yup', I stared back at him.

'What do you expect? Neither of you can paddle a canoe or concentrate when you behave like this. So let's go. I've got dinner to make, unless you guys want to help.'

I raised my eyebrows at them both, smiling. They were quiet. We walked the canoes up the river a hundred metres or so and then where the bank was less steep, launched ourselves and paddled back to the island where the group was gathered in silence.

I was taking no chances. Mary paddled with Odi, and I paddled the other canoe with Carel. Strangely enough, there was silence. All went well.

I delegated duties and made everyone busy preparing the camp. Setting up a bed to show them how we did it. I made them all do their own, and then started dinner preparation. I showed them how to wash out of a bucket away from the waters' edge. No one suggested a quick swim. Dinner was on the go, and a bottle of wine was being poured. I started giggling . . . the image of Odi splashing Carel, and the humour of it all suddenly surfaced, and I started laughing. The two Greeks had stopped talking and were very subdued with each other . . . I laughed and tried to stop, and everyone stared at me. I laughed again and couldn't stop. It was infectious, and the tension was too great. Gotty and Bernhardt, quiet all afternoon, smiled and laughed too, and then the girls and the English boys started politely laughing too. The Greeks eventually smiled and then started too. 'You should have seen those hippos' faces.' I managed eventually, 'They couldn't believe you were heading straight at them,' I carried on. 'Odi, you lost your paddle, you nit . . .' Screams of laughter. 'Paddling with your hands like a friggin' windmill.' More uncontrollable laughter . . . 'You . . .' I pointed at Carel. 'Getting soaked and shouting at Odi . . .' More laughter.

Eventually, we managed to calm down, and we made dinner in a collective aura of peace and good humour. When we gradually all peeled off to bed, there were still a collection of guffaws as one in the group would remember a scene from the chaos of the moment.

The next day was much better, but we still had a *lot* of mileage out of the Greeks as they became known. We made it to Chirundu and then eventually Mana Pools, but not without some more excitement. We had an elephant walk past the camp one night on his way over a sand island to the river. His giant shadow stretched over us, with the steady soft crunch of sand and blow of air through his trunk. A few woke up but remained still in their cocoons of cotton and netting on the sandy bank of the Zambezi.

The Greeks improved markedly after that first day, but were still likely to head off if they weren't thinking. Gotty and Bernhardt got along very well and became cautious if not slow paddlers and regarded every hippo herd with extreme suspicion. The two women had a close shave when as the last canoe one day, I had to bellow at them to paddle hard as a hippo was coming for them. Mary had become really competent and confident and could be relied on to be sensible if hippo popped up too close for comfort and would back off and wait for the hippo to reappear before doing anything. She was so far unflappable. Peter and Mark, the English boys, were steady and reliable, although the one stuttered a little if he was in a conversation for too long. They had a great sense of humour and would pull each others legs unmercifully.

We had been confronted by a single bull hippo who had dared us approach him in a channel. He had stood shoulder-deep and glared at us, biting at the water, snorting and gaping wide-mouthed at the sky. Typical behaviour of a recalcitrant bull.

I had been very gentle with him, stopping well away from him, and watching him from a good distance, I explained to the group what he was doing and why. We would have to paddle several hundred metres back upstream and go far right to carry on. I was hoping we could persuade the hippo to move forty metres downstream to a deeper channel, where we could paddle quietly past him. He would have ample room to feel safe and unthreatened by our canoes. It was four o'clock, and we had a little time. There was no pressure. We waited, and he glared. I talked to him, told him he was being silly and tiresome. He bit the water. I quite understood, and I continued. He was tired of canoes bugging him. He snorted and rump raised, defecated, tail flaying the soft, grassy faeces into the water. This was a territorial display . . . *his* territory.

'OK', I thought, 'we were going to get out and walk the canoes past him.' Hippos prefer to stay in deep waters, and although they may demonstrate and gape, normally they stayed in the water. I gathered the group and told them of my decision. 'We are going to vork past ze 'eepo?' asked Bernhardt, resorting to his vernacular.

I nodded. 'Yup, towing the canoes by the painter.'

'It's OK, we often have to do this. The hippo will back off and go to deep waters. We need to be quick and quiet as he will be under the water, where we cannot see him. It should be fine. Don't worry.'

The group was excited as we hadn't had any real action since that first day. I was cautious as always with these situations. Hippo were big and fast. We would see about five hundred hippos on a five-day safari normally, and provided one was careful and alert, there was a significantly reduced chance of a problem with a hippo that had been seen.

It was generally the one the guide did not see that created the problems.

I started down the edge of the sand bar channel, and the others followed close at my heels, my rifle in one hand and the painter in the other. I told the Greeks to give me about ten-metres distance as we neared the hippo. They were quiet. The sun was very hot. We were all sweating in the heat. Heads all covered with hats of varying shapes and styles.

The hippo snorted and turned away. He started to walk head down downstream away from us. I watched him carefully, then beckoned the group. 'No talking.' They tugged and lead the canoes, only the odd thud as the canoes nosed the bank here and there. The hippo reached deep water and slid away, his bulk absorbed by the water of the river. I watched the broad V shape of his back disappear with the current, and he was gone. I carried on walking and glancing back at my group. They smiled. I smiled, and we carried on. I waited for him to reappear or his broad snout to emerge and to blow spray, before sucking in great breaths of Zambezi air. Nothing. Hippo can hold their breath for up to seven minutes on average, and he still had time. We walked on, the river broadened here, and it was still.

I motioned for everybody to climb in. The hippo had disappeared on the other side of the 'crossroad' about forty-five metres away. Quickly, we climbed in and headed off, hugging the bank. Deep, strong strokes, quietly and quickly we gathered speed and distance. I looked behind me again. All looked good. Gotty and Bernhardt behind me, the Greeks, Peter and Mark and then the girls, Mary and Kate. The Greeks were slowing and looking around, chatting quietly. I watched the water, my senses working. Deciding to risk it, I spoke loudly, 'Move it up there, you lot. We are still in deep waters.' A pun.

The girls had slowed a little to let the other canoe get on, and I saw the hippo rise behind and twenty metre to the right. Silently, he had surfaced, ears waggling to clear the water. 'Mary, that hippo is behind you. You all need to paddle hard *now*,' I spoke urgently to them. They paddled. The Greeks pulled hard, and we all shot out of there at a speed, leaving him staring after us. 'Phew, that was close,' Gotty said. He never said much, except in emphasis. We entered a shallow tree-lined channel, and I paused to see if anything was lurking in the shade. It was a channel I knew well and was often interesting with elephants or game of sorts in the shade of the mahoganies. We drifted and paddled easily down, feeling the tension ease out in the shade. Suddenly, there was a tremendous crash behind me and a woman's scream. I spun around to see clouds of dust and spray and tree leaves.

Backing as fast as I could and avoiding the other two canoes, the Greeks clung to some roots, eyes wide and fixed on the melee behind them. A huge branch had broken off and crashed down just in front of the girls' canoe. I leapt out of my canoe and rushed over to them, leaving my canoe with the Greeks. They were fine. The branch had fallen two metres in front of the prow, giving them both a tremendous fright and covering them in dust and water. Kate shed a few tears and Mary hugged her, both of them looking dust-streaked and waif-like. 'Hey, you two, you gave me a helluva fright. What were you doing, rocking the boat?' I touched them both on their shoulders, they laughed shrilly and sat there gathering their wits. 'You need to get out, and I will pull your boat through this,' I said.

We were a close-knit crew that night in the camp and a glass or two of wine loosened everybody up well. It was our last night together as well. The Chiruwe lions serenaded us for the first part of the evening. It was a good night and a fitting end to a very memorable trip.

Over the years this safari became a 'Must do' and thousands of happy canoeists went down that great river, creating their own memories and adventures too. Some of these stories will be written about in later narratives. True, there were casualties and not every story had a happy ending, but they were a tiny percentage of the man-hours canoe guides spent on that great and significant river.

At the time of writing, people have been canoeing the Zambezi in fibreglass craft for over thirty years. Eddy Rous and John Stevens had no idea what they were starting when Canoeing Safaris (Pvt) Ltd opened business so many years ago!

LEOPARD AND LIONS BY MOONLIGHT

Walking in the Zambezi Valley has always been one of the greatest adventures for any guide. It is one of the very few national parks in Africa, where visitors can walk freely without a guide in a dangerous game area. The open habitat of the flood plain lends itself to walking. The mature winterthorn woodland with its different levels of flood plain, bisected by river gulleys from the old days when the river would flood creating mini rivers through the woodland. This flood plain is what makes Mana so special, and the game to be seen and enjoyed is indeed incredible. Mana Pools was also declared a World Heritage site in the 1980s when an ill-conceived government plan for a dam threatened to destroy this entire area.

(As I review this script now, the valley is again under threat from Chinese mining activities, again with government approval!)

I started doing walks in the park area and used to conduct two night trails from Nyamepi (Mana Pools HQ) down river to Chikwenya, at the junction of the Sapi and Zambezi Rivers. These trails were always exciting, and the game experience outstanding. Elephants dominated the experience normally, and lions would be heard virtually all night. On trail, we all slept on the ground. Each person had their own plastic groundsheet, sometimes a rubber mat as a sleeping mat, a sleeping bag, and made their beds under a mosquito net hung from any suitable branch or from the rope that I would hang to create a sleeping spot under a tree. I would choose a spot that I considered safe and then by dragging thorn branches into a circle and stretch a rope across for the mosquito nets. I preferred to sleep off to one side under my own bush so that I could observe any problems from a different spot should a problem arise.

On a walk from Mana to Chikwenya with two British army officers, Jeremy and Mike, Maggie, Mike's wife, a friend of theirs, Alain, we had some fine experiences.

It was a nice small group and would mean that we could hide and observe animals more easily along the trail. On our first night, I had chosen a spot just down from the Chiruwe River, a sandy river bed, severely braided and covered in a woodland of fever-berry trees and mixed deciduous species. The thickets covering the river course were a safe habitat for lion, leopard, bushbuck, kudu, and, naturally, elephant, apart from a host of other antelopes and smaller predators too. Our spot was open on all sides, and I had chosen to put everybody with heads against a large fever-berry tree with our torsos out like the spokes of a wheel.

We had bathed by scooping water from the river and sponge bathing the sweat off ourselves, then making dinner of pasta and dehydrated soya-based meats. Everybody had eventually peeled off to bed, and I finished my hot chocolate and pushed my faithful mug deep into my pack, inside a plastic bag . . . out of reach of ants.

Gentle snores and quiet gradually stole over the group and a feeling of well-being infused me with sleep. The woodland night noises filled the night. A pair of wood owls duetted in the denser treeline. Lions and hyena squabbled over something far off, and the growls and screams of these predators stirred the sleepers around me. Hippo snorts were a continuous noise along the river. Fish splashes and water thick-knees (a nocturnal bird) completed the river chorus. I settled deeper into my sleeping bag, feeling good. I loved these trails. A leopard called downriver, and I listened happily.

The leopard called again, closer this time. I shifted carefully so that I could see the riverbank, where a faint trail was visible to me from beneath the leaves. We were concealed effectively from outside view by the leaves of the tree drooping around us. I watched the bank, sleep fleeing from my mind as I listened again to the rasping saw of the leopard. I debated about waking the others, but did not want to frighten the cat as I was a little apart from the others, grouped on the other side of the tree trunk. I moved quietly again, my eyes straining to see in the pale light of the moonlight filtered by the canopy of the woodland. Suddenly, the pale shape of the cat appeared walking lithely straight towards our tree. My breath stopped. Here I was on my back with a leopard approaching totally unaware of our presence. It was superb. It was a male with a big head, good sized, and with a cocky attitude. The cat stopped about ten metres from the tree and sniffed the ground. He looked about him, poised and powerful, tail curled showing the white fluff on the underside. I watched in disbelief. The cat squatted and defecated on the path. The strong acrid ammonia cat stench nearly made me cough. Finished, he turned and delicately sniffed the air well above the steaming pile, then proceeded to scrape dust over his dung. A few strokes and that was it. He paused again, eyes dark in the shadows and strolled past our tree, taking the path that slightly bypassed us, an age-old shortcut across a bend in the river.

He called again, the deep rasp sounding even louder and his breathing clear to me. I listened in awe. It took a long time for sleep to claim me that night, and in the morning, the pile of odoriferous evidence was all I needed to substantiate my story. They could not believe that I had watched a *real* leopard walk past them whilst they slept. It was a great start to a trail.

We had a wonderful day that day, following the curve of the original watercourse way inland against the high banks with the deciduous woodlands. Elephant and buffalo we stalked and watched from behind fallen tree stumps along the way. Zebra, impala, and warthog were common. Eland and kudu less so, and we watched them several times from cover as we walked through the woodlands. At one time, we had found a small pan and sat down and enjoyed our lunch of salami, cheese, and biscuits. Talking quietly, we had watched a shy herd of nyala step delicately down to the waters' edge and with ears twitching this way and that, drinking carefully the water and then stepping delicately to disappear into the jesse as silently as they came. We disturbed a couple of spotted hyena's snoozing under some thick bushes. They sat up totally surprised and disbelieving, their big round ears alert and then bolted, turning to look at us as they ran.

That night I chose a large mahogany tree at the start of one of the huge flood plains for our campsite. The moon was pretty full that night, and having missed out on the first night, everybody was wide awake for some time. The dry grass flattened and trampled by animals, formed a wonderful light background for us in the moonlight. Using binoculars we watched two porcupines foraging along the floor of the woodland. Their quills making them appear like big dark clouds apart from the faint grunts and growls they made from time to time. A group of hyena wandered past, shifty and hunchbacked in a silent and deadly ninja-pack, their heads bobbing and staring as they watched us, silently watching them. They had wandered up to within twenty metres from us, before stopping and staring at such an unusual collection. I didn't want them hanging around, so scattered them with a well-thrown stick, and they scuttled off leaving a pall of fine dust hanging in the air for some minutes. Lions started roaring at one stage, the roars carrying up the river and echoing around the tall, gracious woodland, a wonderful amphitheatre. Everyone had gone to bed, and at the first roar, three of them had come over to me, and we sat together against the solid trunk of the mahogany, waiting and listening. The calls varied slightly. There were three cats, and we heard that. Two sounded similar, but the third had a longer, deeper voice, and he tailed off with more grunts than the others. I checked where my rifle was, and the load too. Soft-nosed rounds were more effective on lion than hard-nosed rounds. Not that I expected to even worry about it, but it was an automatic response. I knew lions.

We waited. It seemed that the entire woodland waited. It was *so* quiet. Our senses were completely on edge, and we scanned the area with binoculars. On moonlit nights, binoculars worked very well, and we had watched several mongoose as well as the porcupines going about their business. Mike was scanning quietly, Maggy firmly beside him. Jeremy and I sat facing more forwards, on the ground, half hidden behind two big branches that formed part of our barricade. Alain was still tucked in his sleeping bag . . . twitching every time the lions roared. A muffled voice had asked me how close they really were . . . when I told him he said in a strangled voice, 'Oh no . . .'! We watched . . . and suddenly, they were right in front of us. They were almost ghostly in the grey light of the moon. Through the binoculars, yellow eyes staring, their manes hung like shadows about their massive heads.

I will never forget their stance. They had been walking in line when they had seen us. They stopped and stared as only a lion can – directly. One of them started roaring, their noise reverberating right through me, and their resonance shaking my very core. The figure in the sleeping bag quivered and shrunk even more into the foetal curl.

We sat and watched them, totally, awestruck by the magnificence of the moment. I think everybody had stopped breathing. Not another sound was to be heard.

One of them strolled up to a snowberry bush and rubbed his head on the low straggly branches, walked against the bush, and then sprayed it. Little jets of disdain sprayed against the bush. He stared again at us and led the trio away and past us. The other two finished roaring. Their hoarse, belly grunts fading away into the night. Stillness. We watched . . . they paused a moment longer, tails flicking in annoyance, the dark tips dancing in the light before they too disappeared into the moon-grey light of the bush. None of us moved, storing the encounter in our minds. I scanned the woodland scrub again, nothing. Somebody swallowed noisily, and Alain shifted in his sleeping bag breaking the spell.

'Wasn't that incredible!' I turned to the others . . . they looked dumbstruck. Mike and Maggie were shoulder to shoulder on their knees, peering over the log right behind Jeremy and me. 'Absolutely bloody awesome!' they murmured.

'I need a wee . . . , Mike?' Maggie nudged her husband.

'OK, OK . . . give me a mo',' he answered.

'Don't worry, we won't go far.'

The lions roared again . . . further away and slightly muted now as they faced upriver and challenged the intruders upstream. Maggie hesitated, 'It's OK,' I reassured her, 'they are a way away from us now. Just pop behind that little shrub over there.'

'Don't worry, we aren't going anywhere,' Mike answered.

'Just here will be fine.' They moved to the edge of the tree shadow.

We had one further leopard encounter on this walk, which was unusual, and this time we didn't even know he had been there. I found the noxious little pile a bare fifteen metres from my bivvy one morning and tracked his footprints to the scrub line a short distance away.

PAINTED DOGS AND ELEPHANTS VISITING

One of my other walks along the river was equally memorable by some very different experiences. Mana Pools is a unique national park in Zimbabwe, and visitors may walk freely along the flood plains and in the woodlands with care as the wildlife there is not tame or habituated, but certainly generally visible. When I used to do the trails there, I never encountered other people walking through the denser and less frequented areas downstream of Nyamepi (the Park HQ) and so my guests did not feel that they were in populated park.

The habitat varied enormously depending on the soils and geology of the particular zone we were walking over. Way downstream of Mana, the mopane forest forms a loose canopy woodland, where the golden dry grass carpets the shadow scattered floor of the woodland. This woodland is quiet except for the fork-tailed drongos and hornbills, which are large and visible. Occasional flocks of white helmet shrikes drift through, their black-and-white plumage a brief flash to an observer. Only the buzz and bite of tsetse flies caused me a problem.

I had stopped in a particularly pretty area and wearily eased my pack off, leaning it against a mopane log, reclining at the perfect height for me to sit and was suggesting a tea break. Through the woodland the low, hooting calls of a painted dog alerted us, and I shushed everyone to listen. Everybody froze, looking expectantly at me . . . 'Wild dogs!' I stage whispered, smiling with great excitement. Quickly gathering everybody and dropping their packs, we moved slowly forward to where we had a clear view across and through the trees towards the sound. Silence. The heat was already oppressive, and only the cicada's incessant buzzing pulsed in our ears. There it was again . . . '*Woooo, wooo, woooo* . . .' a soft and low-frequency call that carried to the round, black ears of the pack somewhere . . . We crouched down for a better look, and there they were.

Two dogs stood looking towards us. Incredible! My walkers looked nervous, and I had to reassure them that the dogs were totally harmless to man. 'Look, I'll try to call them over . . .'

'What . . . no we don't need to stroke them.' Huge alarm in their faces. I laughed and rolled my eyes.

'No, don't worry. They aren't *that* obliging. Come and sit quietly.'

I squatted next to a tree trunk and pursed my lips, imitating their contact call. The two dogs did a double take and then trotted towards us, stopped, and then continued for a few more steps. They were about thirty metres away now and watching us cautiously. Dark eyes bright, large rounded black ears, the blotched yellow-and-black coats daubed with splashes of white made them unique as animals. Only the bottom half of the tail in all individuals is white . . . a flag when they are excited.

I sat down, motioning to my four walkers to do the same . . . bottoms on the ground. We sat and stared at them. They stared at us, heads alert and curious. I called again . . . one dog trotted forward, head and shoulders level, interested. It stopped about ten metres away from us, nose working, collecting our scent. It gave a little barking growl, an alert, and bounded back a few paces before turning to look at us again, still wary, but less tense. The other dog was staring off into the distance, ears cocked and then loped away on tireless legs. The second dog paused and followed. We watched them until they were out of sight amongst the rough-barked silent trees.

'We are *so* lucky,' I enthused. 'Wild or more correctly, Painted dogs are an endangered species here, and to see them here is fantastic. What a pleasure!'

My walkers were slightly less sure this was a good thing.

'Why aren't they dangerous to us?' one of the women asked.

'We aren't a typical prey for them. They are just curious about us. If you run, they will follow you, for sure. But it's because they can . . . there is no record of dogs ever attacking humans. People have run away from them and climbed trees . . . and said they were chased. Absolute bull. When you climb a tree, it gives the dogs "space" to come closer and look at you, get your scent, so they do. If you are frightened, then it's intimidating, but they will soon get bored and lie down or go away.' I went on. 'I have often crawled up to dogs and sat with them for ages as they dozed. As long as you move slowly and treat them gently, they will tolerate you. When they have had enough, they will move away from you. I once had twenty-two dogs around me in Hwange . . . all sniffing, and they got bored very quickly and wandered off to snooze. It was incredible.'

Exhilarated by our encounter, we forgot about 'tea' and gathering our packs, carried on. Later on, we watched several impala, eyes terrified, wide, bounding past us, and stotting, bouncing with a stiff-legged rocking-horse gait, their hoarse breathing loud, and that's how close they were to us. 'The dogs are hunting them . . . that's why they are running like that,' I spoke quietly, hoping we would see those big ears appear again. 'It's called stotting . . . and they seem to do it only when the dogs are after them.' We paused a few minutes in the shade of a large tamarind tree, hoping to see the dogs, and then continued.

That evening we camped near the river again, just off the plains. I selected a spot where the deeply eroded bank formed a natural and comforting obstacle on the two sides so we could block the remaining approach from the landside easily. After a comfortable meal and coffee, we had gradually settled down and were drifting off under a clear night sky. Only the butterfly-wing outline of the mopane leaves were clear to me as I succumbed to the feeling of well-being and slept.

Sometime in the night, I rose quickly from oblivion, my senses alerted by a presence. I lay there, listening intently . . . tense. Soft breathing sounds and movement came to me . . . a rasping brushing sound, and the sound of earth being brushed by something along the hippo trail below and next to me. A stick cracked in front of me and the sound of leaves being stripped told me that an elephant, no

. . . maybe several elephants were feeding near us. A soft, deep bubbling resonance filled my ears . . . elephant talk. I relaxed and smiled to myself. I wondered how the rest of my group was doing. I had put my bed towards the front of the group, on one of the smaller 'spits', a little apart from Jeremy, Mike, and Maggie. Alain was on the other side of the main spit. I heard his sleeping bag being zipped up and shuffling . . . the elephants all stopped feeding. Silence.

Then they carried on, and I could hear several different animals feeding now, in front and to the sides of our group. One animal's head and ears were silhouetted against the stars in my vision . . . it leant against the flimsy barricade at my feet, its long flexible, twin-finger-tipped trunk stretching out for the fresh shoots on a straggly mopane bush next to me. I watched as the 'fingers' grasped the stick and deftly stripped the few leaves off, curling carefully inwards to stop them falling. Wondering what it was going to do as I was clearly in the way . . . I watched in some trepidation. The animal realised that it couldn't, shouldn't walk over my pack and comatose form, shook its ears loudly and turned away.

There was a whole herd, and we were in the way. I sat up quietly to try and assess what our situation was . . . Nobody had moved a muscle, apart from Alain . . . The herd, the cows, and the calves were all feeding happily and contented, crunching and deep exhalations of elephant breath were all I could hear. Then I heard the deep 'thump' of faeces falling and a stream of urine over to my right. Thump . . . thump . . . thump . . . the strong stench of ammonia and elephant dung flooded my senses. I suppressed the desire to giggle and grinned into the darkness, imagining my companion's fears and feelings at all this. These elephants were right amongst us. Whatever everybody was feeling now, we did not want the animals to get a fright as somebody was bound to get injured as the animals panicked and ran.

I lay and listened to the herd as it gradually moved away from 'our' spot, the periodic cracking of branches and sound of stripping leaves became gradually fainter, and I slept. The continuous hippo chorus from the river had almost become a 'non-invasive' background noise, and distant roars of Zambian lions faded in and out of my consciousness. It was the harsh crowing of a Swainson's spurfowl that woke me as the light filtered through the mopane woodland. It was always a wonderful way to start a day . . . Just to lie there for a while knowing that my only responsibility that day was to ensure we had a safe walk, with only the herds of elephants and the occasional buffalo bulls to be negotiated before we camped for our last evening near the Chitembe River. Eventually, I rose and put water on my stove for tea. Jeremy and Mike were stirring, and I took my small hand towel and wandered down to the river to find a 'safe spot' to wash my face and do my teeth.

That day was a fine walk, and the mopane trees sheltered us as we walked through the dappled light, our footsteps muffled by the ankle-high golden stems of the *Chloris* and other grasses. Periodic flocks of white helmet shrikes twittered and chorused prettily as we disturbed their monastic existence in the woodland. The ever present pert black forms of fork-tailed drongos perched on the edge of trees, watched us closely, their deep red eyes beady with intent in case we disturbed insects for them to hawk deftly around us as we walked.

At one point, a herd of buffalo had slept the night in the trees. The large smooth flattened patches of grass were punctuated with extra large dung pats, indicating that these were early morning 'deposits' as they were larger than normal. The herd had moved off undisturbed down to the riverside, their large cloven hoofs cutting deeply into the soft sand and then the muddy edge, to drink deeply from the river. I anticipated catching up with them during the day. We would undoubtedly find some of the old bulls at the back of the herd, or the clouds of cattle egrets that invariably followed these large herds around would reveal their position. I remarked on this to my companions. They looked nervous, but as we weren't walking in thick bush, I wasn't too concerned.

By lunchtime, we had the top of Chikwenya Island in sight and the Chitembe River was marked by the dark line of the riverine trees along its course. I heard the low belly grunt of a buffalo . . . stopped and motioned to the others with my hand. Stop. Scanning the bush carefully I eventually found a dark shape of a buffalo. The horns were still and low, an animal lying down contentedly ruminating . . . cheeks moving slowly in an age-old rhythm .' We watched for a moment. Silent. 'Let's go back a way and give them some space. I don't want to disturb them now'. We filed away from the river. The wind was in my favour, so I was not worried about our scent being carried to them.

We walked back and about a kilometre from the herd, we found a great big shady tree. We spent the rest of the afternoon near there as I was certain the herd wasn't going to move far.

That night my only worry was the likely chance of lions walking through our camp on the hunt for the buffalo, so we made sure we had a 'good' barricade of thorns around us.

SNAKE BITE ON A WALK . . . A WICKED LESSON TAUGHT!

In Zimbabwe, people coming on safari are often deeply concerned about seeing or worse still being bitten or 'confronted' by a snake. The truth is that nine out of ten safaris do not ever see a snake, let alone have a chance to be bitten by one. More commonly, the guides or trackers will see the snake and because we all know how unnerved most western Europeans are by this, we fail to say anything until we are better acquainted with our guests and know if the snake will be appreciated or not.

I had an occasion to use a snake to my own ends during a rather trying and arduous half-day walk, with some very tiresome South-African youths and their parents. This family had been on a three-day experience with an ex-national park's individual, who had made the most of their naivety and filled their heads with all sorts of misinformation, and in so doing, had also made a huge impression on the four youths who now thought they were next in-line for their guides' licenses. Naturally, I was not impressed, but rather concerned at this rather unfortunate state of affairs and the effect it had on these young men. Misinformation was worse than no information.

During the morning's walk, I had been questioned and deliberately set-up a number of times, and in front of the parents had my own abilities questioned quite disdainfully by these 'new' heroes. So an opportunity presented itself quite unexpectedly to test them.

We were having a short break, sitting on a log, deep in a teak forest somewhere in the Makololo area, in Hwange. I had grown quite weary of the attitude that now presented itself from the boys and was chatting with the parents who were very pleasant and appeared to be enjoying a chance to talk about matters not related to wildlife. I spotted a large yellow-bellied sand snake sunning itself in the leaf litter just a few metres away from where we were sitting, and immediately announced my intention to catch the fellow and talk about him. This species is common and widespread in the whole region, and as they were South Africans, thought this might be interesting and save a snake's life sometime in the future.

The boys were told where to stand in a semi-circle to block his escape . . . deep consternation from the two of them and disbelief from the other two. 'Quickly, you guys . . . stand there, and there . . . and don't let him through. They are lightening fast.'

'What . . . what if he bites?'

'They are only mildly poisonous, don't worry. Didn't Stanley tell you that?'

They barely had time to digest this information when I had approached the copse where the snake was and stalking him quickly, I pounced . . . carefully avoiding damaging him, but trapping him beneath some small sticks and leaves as he slid away. I lifted my one hand to grip the snake, and there was far more of him than I had bargained for. His head appeared to one side and he swung around and bit me behind the knee in the fleshy part of the tendon. His small, but determined, head was wide open as he chewed and chewed on my flesh. Gasps of horror from all around me. I carefully grasped him behind the head, and he immediately tried to let go of his grip and bite my hand instead. His teeth were stuck in my leg . . . he wriggled his head more and his teeth came unstuck. Gaping fiercely, he tried to turn his head, but I had him firmly, but safely. Rising to my feet and looping his beautifully patterned body in my left hand, I enthused over 'our' capture. 'Just look at this fellow . . . his colour is fantastic . . . canary yellow belly, white stripes, and caramel colouring. His eyes are orange and slightly forward facing. See . . . I offered the snake to my audience.' No one moved. In fact, there had been no sound at all . . . I looked up at them. They were staring at me . . . shocked and worried.

The boys were staring at me by now and my blood-oozing leg . . . the snake had left a double row of small lacerations, which were bleeding quite profusely. All bravado had fled . . . one looked a little white. The mother was holding her hand in front of her mouth and looking at my leg too. The father looked at the snake and then me. 'Are you OK?' he asked. 'Sure,' I answered, . . . 'absolutely fine.' I smiled, looking him straight in the eyes. A wicked scheme came to my mind.

'OK, anybody wants to hold him or to touch him. He's fine now, and will be calm in a moment now that he knows I'm not going to harm him.' I offered the squirming snake to the boys . . . 'Come on, guys, he won't hurt you now.' I offered the eldest and most disdainful brother the snake. He looked at me in horror and backed off as did the others. The father offered his hands. 'Can I just feel it?'. I held the snake's body and draped it over his smooth hands. His fingers stroked and touched the sleek cool form, feeling the smooth muscles and scales. It was a large yellow belly, and he was still very agitated, so I did not offer to have him hold it as one so commonly can with a newly caught one of this species. 'Well, it certainly isn't slimy or cold!' the father exclaimed, smiling. He looked at his wife, and she exclaimed and backed off hurriedly. 'OK,' I said, 'let's give him his freedom, shall we?' I moved off a few metres and released the snake. He slithered a few inches and then confident once more moved rapidly away. Gone, back into his snake world.

I paused and then slumped to the ground . . . one leg twitching spasmodically . . . rustling the leaves. 'Look out, he's collapsed!' There was bedlam. 'I told you he's going to die and look . . . look he's collapsed.' Alarm and despondency spread like a bad smell at the dining table. The boys started shouting at each other and at the father. The mother shouted at the father and at the boys. One of them said, 'Which way's the vehicle . . . ?' Answer. 'I don't know . . . It's there. No, it isn't. It's over there.' The boys started arguing over who was right . . . The father was trying to calm them down, and the mother was arguing with him. I lay and listened for a while . . . noticing that nobody had come near me. Now there were two lots of shouting, and I could hear someone crying. One of the boys was laughing. The others were at a complete loss as to what to do. I thought I'd done enough, so I groaned and twitched the leg again. Silence . . . and three came over to me.

I opened my eyes and slowly stood up, brushing the leaf litter off me. There was a sudden silence as all eyes were on me. I nonchalantly gathered my gear, and said, 'OK, let's go. It's getting late.' I left my blood-soaked leg alone deliberately. It wasn't that sore, and I deliberately didn't want to attend to it unnecessarily.

'Are you OK?' the father asked.

'Sure, I'm fine,' I answered him, smiling at him. 'I was just interested to see which way the boys here would take you if I did fall by the wayside.' I grinned at him.

'It seems as though they had forgotten all that bush-knowledge that Stanley filled them with . . . instead of keeping cool and calm, and being rational. I also notice that no one actually came to see if I was OK . . .' I paused, 'Surely, the best way of finding your way home . . .'. I smiled at the father to take the sting out of it. He looked at me for a moment and then smiled. Man to man, he understood. The mother was not so forgiving and had a thundercloud look. I didn't look at the boys . . .

We walked on, and I chatted on as though nothing had happened. All I could hear behind me was mutterings and then heavy silences . . . and more mutterings. When I did turn around to point out things of interest, the boys avoided my eyes and hung their heads. The father was fine, but the mother wasn't. She was still very put out. Life's like that sometimes.

It was a lesson learnt, and they were pleasant enough the next day when they left.

I was not in the habit of making people look fools, and I never did it just for the sheer fun of it, but I did it to make cocky youngsters less sure of themselves, especially if they were being obnoxious and superior. I will recall another story when I used a little license to teach some kids a small and harmless lesson.

I was leading a canoeing and camping trip in Mana Pools, Zimbabwe, with a family from Connecticut. The parents, John and Carol, had brought their three youngsters along with them and the youngest was just on twelve years of age, our preferred minimum age for walking on a safari.

We had spent a really fun few days, but the eldest son was a bully at times and could get very personal and had started to get familiar and cocky when we were out on a drive or a walk. He had started to get blasé about animals and had once refused to listen when I told them all to sit quietly as an elephant wandered past. Not good, and the father had been embarrassed by his son's rudeness. I said little and was fair in my brief comment.

The next morning was our last walk. We had heard lion way up the back near the mopane, and I thought we might have a chance if we walked through before driving up to the airfield and seeing them off. As we walked along, I saw that a cowherd of elephant had walked that way a few hours before us and left a few moist droppings in their wake. I stopped and examined the dung for seeds and leaves out of honest curiosity. The eldest son pushed forward. 'Don't you know that its elephant dung?' he spoke aggressively and tried to be funny. 'Sure,' I said, smiling. 'Bull or cow?' I asked. He stared at me and then at the large odious balls of straw-coloured moistness that already had a beetle or two crawling around it. 'Come on then.' Still smiling, and wanting him to get it right. 'Bull or cow?' The multiple spoors were only visible with careful scrutiny as the pathway was hard-packed. The other two stooped and chattered excitedly, pointing out this and that. The parents were helping them. I stooped and shoved my forefinger deep into the pile. Wiggled it. Paused a moment. Pulled it out and shoved my second finger deep into my mouth . . . gazed into the distance as in deep thought . . . pulled it out. 'Cow, two calves at foot, probably fifteen years old . . .' I focused on the boy's face. It was incredulous. His eyes were staring at me, at the smudge of elephant dung on my cheek from my finger and knuckles . . . 'You didn't!' I smiled and said nothing. 'It's a cow,' I said, 'with calves. Look let's look at the spoor.' He stared at me, disbelief and uncertainty in his eyes. His sister grabbed him and said, 'He did . . . look at his finger and his mouth.' They all looked at me now. The mother put her hand to her mouth, horrified. 'Gavin, what did you do?'

I was nonchalant. 'Well, sometimes you have to feel it to see how warm it is,' I answered. 'But you tasted it as well?'. 'That's a sure way to sex it, if you aren't sure' . . . I paused.

By now, the sister was hissing at her brother, 'Yes, he *did*. I saw it. Now *you* do it . . . smartipants!' She had been the brunt of much of his attitude recently and was an unwitting ally. 'No, YOU DON'T', came from the mother, angry.

The father said nothing, not being certain. The smell of elephant dung was strong around us. I carried on talking about the seeds and leaves, moving the dung with a forefinger.

Suddenly, the elder son shoved his finger deep into the dung, and before the parents could do anything, he put it into his mouth and held it there for a moment.

He looked confused and took it out, spitting as he did so. The mother let out a small shriek and put her hands to her mouth again. The two siblings just stared and started to laugh. 'What does it taste like?' they asked, standing right in front of him and looking into his face. 'What does it taste like?' Again, I looked at him, smiling a little . . . 'So what do you think?' I moved away so that they couldn't see my face. The father now spoke up . . . 'Gavin didn't put his finger in his mouth, you chump. He put his other finger in his mouth . . . like this,' he demonstrated and stood shaking his head. 'Here, wash your mouth out a little.' I offered him a bottle of water. The siblings screamed with laughter as only children can, going over and over the scene in their minds . . . The mother was furious and scolded me for leading her son on, and the father just laughed.

The boy looked crestfallen and washed his mouth out a few times, laughing ruefully as he did so. 'Well done,' I said to him, 'you were really brave, but you didn't need to put your finger in your mouth to see that it was a cow. All you had to do was look carefully at the spoor here. Look here . . .' I showed him the faint, lacey track of the adult and the smaller footprints scuffed next to them. 'Remember, we talked about tracking yesterday'.

Once, they were all over it, we carried on walking with gusts of laughter every now and then from the kids. I couldn't stop smiling all day.

Oh, what fun we had on safari! Each day was challenge, something new to see, sort out and embrace.

BUFFALO AND BRUISES

The canoeing in those days was very different to what guests experience nowadays. The river is the same, and all that has physically changed is the course of the river a little here and there, and the islands too have moved or become vegetated. Small changes brought about by the flow and load of the seasons. There was a funny incident when a certain well-known guide was doing a lot of canoeing as a free lance guide. I will let Alistair tell this story himself!

```
"In the early 1990's I was conducting a backed-up canoe trail from
Ruckomechi Camp to Acacia Point in the Sapi Safari Area. It was
about mid-morning on the third and final day of the trip, whilst
canoeing down a narrow channel in an area known by some guides as
"Little Okavango" when we sighted a herd of approximately seventy
buffalo. Most of the herd were standing on the left side of the
channel close to the water whilst the rest of the herd (about
twenty) were standing on the right side of the channel, also close
to the water.
```

This presented a wonderful photographic opportunity for my guests as these buffalo were fairly habituated to people and could be viewed and photographed at hoof-eye level. We drifted past the main herd on the left during which time my guests got some excellent photos and video footage. After we had drifted past the buffalo, I decided to do a U-turn and approach the rest of the herd on the opposite bank. As we approached them they trotted off a short distance inland. At this point I thought it would be great if I could persuade the buffalo to gallop across the channel to join the rest of the herd on the opposite bank and in so doing, give my guests an opportunity to film and photograph the spectacle. I pulled my canoe in, disembarked and started to walk parallel to the buffalo. To my disappointment, they decided to gallop off in the opposite direction to which I wanted them to go. I broke into a run and tried to head them off hoping that they would change direction and head back in the direction of the rest of the herd which were still in their original position on the other side of the channel. After I had run about fifty metres or so, the buffalo, which at this point were about one hundred metres from me and going at a full gallop, suddenly changed direction and came straight for me in a tightly bunched group with the lead cow in the middle and half a buffalo's length in front of the rest of them. Needless to say at his point I also changed direction and proceeded to sprint away from them, my intention being to attempt to dive into the water of a smaller channel a short distance away as this afforded the only means of escape in an area devoid of trees, termite mounds or anything else that could be used to hide behind. The spectacle can be imagined, a professional guide running like an ostrich possessed, followed by twenty buffalo tightly packed at a full gallop and gaining on him very quickly. The hoof beats got louder and louder and it was not long before I realised that I would not be able to escape them. When the buffalo were about ten metres from me, I turned around and faced them, quickly realising that the only way I would survive this would be to throw myself flat onto the boggy ground, hopefully avoiding a buffalo running off with my entrails wrapped around its horns! In no time the buffalo were on to me, the lead cow swiping at me, connecting the outer curve of her horn onto my forehead but luckily not stopping to work me over. At this point I was a bit dazed and with my face buried in the mud, felt hooves pounding my back and a sharp pain in my left elbow. Just as I was beginning to think what it must be like to be dead, the weight was off my back and I heard the very welcome sound of departing hoof beats. At this stage the most painful thing was a huge lump on my forehead from the cow's horn, but my elbow which was dislocated, was also painful. I half raised my body out of the mud, straightened my left elbow which caused the joint to pop back into place. My immediate concern was to know the whereabouts of the buffalo as I was worried that they would return to finish me off! I saw them standing facing me about eighty metres away and not knowing what their intention was, decided to stay where I was in the prone position, hoping they would move off which thankfully they did after a few minutes. I pulled myself out of the mud and staggered off in the direction of the canoes where I was greeted by a prostrate form on the ground. This prostrate form which was moving convulsively and emitting strange choking noises turned out to be my learner guide Mike Pelham, who was in serious need of oxygen replenishment as he was laughing so much from the spectacle he had just witnessed! Thankfully my guests did not witness the incident as the river was particularly low at the time and they were sitting waiting in their canoes with cameras etc for "the great crossing" which never happened and could not see over the bank.

A.J. Hull

Naturally, the story got out soon enough, and his fellow guides pulled his leg endlessly. Screams of laughter would issue from where we were gathered during the telling of the story. It was one of the great stories of the year, and the hoof-shaped bruises on his back were painful testimony to it all.

MORE FROM THE MATUSADONA

The Cape or Savanna buffalo is a massive and impressive animal. They are often related in stories abounding in danger, drama, and often death. I know that more professional hunters get run over by buffalo (normally wounded) and scratched or mauled by leopard than any other dangerous animals. Buffalo are very difficult to kill when they are full of adrenalin; whether or not they have been wounded, it takes a bullet through the braincase to stop them or a series of heavy calibre bullets in the heart and chest to put them down. I have been fortunate never to have been in the position of danger like that and have killed many buffalo in the course of training guides and backing up during the proficiency tests.

However, they remain one of my most favourite animals and show such presence when they are feeling mean and out of sorts. They can truly show an attitude and give one the creeps when they are watching you on foot. On the other hand, in the heydays of the early eighties, we used to have huge herds of buffalo on the shoreline of the Matusadona National Park, and we could approach these herds with relative lack of concern, as they were used to vehicles and people behaving themselves. I could put my tea box on my shoulder and walk into the middle of a herd of five or six hundred and make tea, all the while being closely observed by the herd, who would, after about five minutes, lie down and relax or carry on feeding. I had an old bull come and lie down on the back of the termite mound of which I was sitting with my group, making flapjacks! Those same guests still mention that adventure to this day when we are sitting in their plush home in New York City!

Incredible but true.

Some might say careless etc. . . . but we were careful to read any 'bad' body language and stay clear if that was observed.

Regrettably, those wonderful large herds no longer exist in the Matusadona. Several years of high water levels wiped out the grazing and excessive lion numbers, and a warden who had a penchant for shooting buffalo for 'training' his scouts all contributed to their demise. Now it is a treat to see a buffalo in the Matusadona. How we loved those big herds! What a true privilege to have lived with them! In summer, we counted herds of over a thousand at a time, and in winter, these would break up into smaller herds as food was scarcer and long lines would wind along the shoreline in search of better grass.

They also learnt to wade into the lake and feed on the water weeds and submerged grasses, bending their heads into the water up to their ears. Quite a sight!

The Matusadona has many ghosts along its shores of rhino, elephant, men, and buffalo that have died along its shores from the time when the lake was filling.

Once, I very nearly disturbed four black rhino lying together at the top of a mountain pathway. I stopped my trailists, and we manoeuvred carefully around them at huge cost to our time schedule and knees, as we slipped and slid around a steep slope to be able to see them better, before we carried on to our rendezvous on the lake shore that afternoon. I presumed they were an adult cow with possibly two of her calves, naturally several years apart, and another young female who had joined them for a while. I would watch herds of elephant feeding along the sides of the hills amongst the sparse Miombo woodlands, scaling the steep slopes that surprised everybody with me at their agility.

We found a spotted hyena 'den' once, high up in a steep-sided gulley, amongst the rocks. It was a complete surprise because we seldom heard hyenas from the camp, and only infrequently saw their dog-like spoor (footprints) on the game trails of the flatlands. They were far more common in the highland areas, as were porcupines, judging by their fibre-filled faeces on the trails. Leopard were rarely seen, but they saw us long before we saw them, and their neat-footed spoor and twice, the warmth of their spotted, lithe bodies could be felt where they had lain a minute before I happened along and disturbed them. Their harsh saw-like rasping calls would be heard once in a while during the early mornings as the dawn light bled the starlight away. The beauty of the Matusadona was in the wilderness feeling, knowing it was not frequently visited by people.

Sure, the shoreline was well traversed, and the bays and inlets were often sites for the large boats to anchor in, and of course, sport fishermen in their small power boats were often in the inlets as well. But the lake shore was an obstacle course of dead trees that had been submerged by the rising waters of the dam in the 1960s. Relatively speaking, the shoreline was undisturbed except for the school holidays when the lake suddenly became inundated with boats and holiday-makers.

At night, the only disturbance was the fleet of 'kapenta rigs' or sardine fishing boats which fished using a bright light suspended over the water. Under the light would be a huge round net that would be drawn up when the shoals of fish had been drawn to the light. Ingenious, but noisy, and the only time they were quiet was over the full moon period, when the fish would not be caught by the artificial light. 'Kapenta' is the local name for the Tanganyika sardine which was introduced into Lake Kariba to create a fishing industry after the creation of the lake.

An early indication of a lifelong passion...Birds in the Encyclopedia Britannica

Learning about nature....Kenya, 1958

Chikwenya was located at the junction of the sandy Sapi and Zambezi rivers

The author lead many wilderness trails through the Matusadona and Mana Pools National Parks

One of my groups on the lip of the escarpment, of the Matusadona,
overlooking lake Kariba

A dramatic kariba sky

A typical lakeshore scene with a grazing elephant

Buffalo were part of our everyday lives

Typical Kariba sunset with dead trees in the water

Rob & Sandy Fynn built Fothergill Island safari camp

Fothergill Island before the water levels dropped sufficiently for us to drive over to the mainland. Circa 1983

Chikwenya, on the banks of the Zambezi. It is a very different place today.

Chikwenya. Brunch on the 'Go'

Chikwenya fire place. Guests watching something over the Sapi river bed, looking into Mana Pools. Jeff Stutchbury is center in long socks.

A very young Dave Winhall standing at the bar!

Ronnie the rhino ambling past the author on the edge of camp.

A Pels fishing owl feather. In those days, a wonderful find on a walk

A Chikwenya bull on the flood plain at camp

Chikwenya. Breakfast interrupted

Mana Pools. Golden light filtering down through the trees

Nyala bulls and females are so different in colour. This group are coming out of the jesse thickets to drink at this pan

Mana Pools. Buffalo herd resting in the morning.

Lions gave me moments of concern at night

Lion spoor is so distinctive
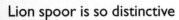
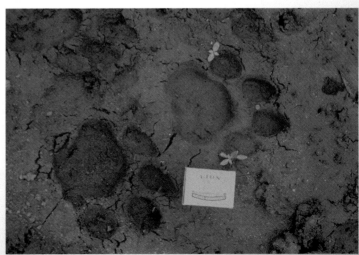

Lion cubs are really cute until you disturb their mother on a walk...then she wants to eat you!

The cheetah boys wandered along the flood plain, giving us all a great thrill!

Dwarf mongoose are common in the Valley, particularly in dry
mopane country

Lions are beautiful predators. Very different to deal with on foot during
the day, compared with night time!

- 'Stretch' A.J. Ferreira, one of my
oldest friends. A passionate guide and
a fierce protector of Mana Pools.

Stretch canoeing two guests at Mana on an afternoon canoe trip

In recent years painted dogs have been seen more frequently along the Zambezi flood plain. They may be approached with slow and careful movements

Painted dogs enjoy a better reputation now, even though they are still persecuted outside of national parks!

A Rock python resting in a small thornbush after I had lifted her out of a puddle of water, where she had been asleep.

The cow and her calf ran across us down the ridge and away...thank goodness!

We disturbed this Black rhino as he was having a mud bath

I once surprised a big Matusadona lion, snoozing all by himself on the edge of the thickets on the lake shore

A rare shot of a dry season Matusadona leopard!

A typical scene of the flood plain at Mana in the dry season. Come the rains it is
a totally different habitat!

An elephant 'Standing tall', watching my approach

This male Yellow baboon jumped up and caught an immature Spurwing goose as it flew over his head. He killed it and then proceeded to eat it.

Chunks of flesh in his mouth

A young female baboon came forward when he had left it momentarily. He struttered back, eyelids flicking in a threat and chased her off

Somewhere in the Matusadona
mountains at a spring.

Photo: Dr. Peter Farrant

Photo: Dr. Peter Farrant

Taking a break in the shade

Trig Point. Matusadona. Chris Sewell in green jacket. Author behind him.
Others unknown

Photo: Dr. Peter Farrant

On trail in the Matusadona. The author with Dr. Peter Farrant on the
Nyamuni river

Photo: Dr. Peter Farrant

Leopard drinking at night. They move absolutely silently and will pass by you like a shadow of the moonlight

This shows how high the leopard went, and then stayed there for the whole day until the lion had finished the impala and left!

Leopard are not always as relaxed as this!

Photo: Jeremy Broad

On trail in the Zambezi Valley, next to one of the islands below Mana

Photo: Jeremy Broad

Elephant are daily sights, and being able to sit quietly with them is common

Photo: Jeremy Broad

Night stop. Mosquito nets strung from a fallen tree suffice

Photo: Jeremy Broad

The last stretch before entering the mopane woodland and then Chikwenya

Sunset on the Zambezi. What a great privilege to be there!

LET SLEEPING RHINO LIE

Black rhino were common at one time in the Matusadona National Park, and during the middle 1980s, when I was doing a lot of trails, they were an animal that was always a thrill to find. Their large grey bird-speckled forms evoked a spurt of adrenaline when I would suddenly come upon them during a walk or on the trail with a pack on my back.

Sometimes the sighting was peaceful (generally one-sided), and at other times, it wasn't!

The best times were when I would sit in a tree, a short distance from a favoured mud wallow, and watch them while they snorted and squealed at each other, like armoured pigs, heaving their huge forms around in the mud and breathing great sighs of satisfaction when they had got it just right and had a few minutes to themselves. The literature states that they are solitary creatures, which they seemed to be, but when it came to a mud wallow or watering point, I often would see two or individuals (normally cows) in close proximity and sometimes even drinking together. They might then sniff each other warily and wander off in different directions, pausing to scrape and spray in a midden along the game trail.

The bulls had an air of menace about them when there was a cow at the mud hole, and invariably she would put her ears back, snort loudly, and back off mewing in 'rhino talk'. The bull would advance cautiously, tail curled and snort, spraying urine at the same time.

There were several meetings with rhino that are still clear in my mind.

I had taken two friends on a trail into the mountains, and we were on our way to Trig Point Spring, a popular watering point for game and me, which was in a fold in the hills just below the trig point slopes, naturally. I was carrying a small day pack as we were camped on the first ridge several kilometres away from the main ridge of the escarpment. We had walked across a wide grassland in the dip between the ridges, and there was no sign of any game around and only scattered small trees. It was late morning and hot. We walked along, just enjoying the wilderness and not speaking at all. The waist-high grass waved in the slight breeze, swishing as we waded through it, leaving a pathway of leaning stalks behind us.

I paused on the edge of a steep gulley which had a stream at the bottom. The rocky sides were almost a wall, and as I peered down into it, we disturbed a rhino which had been hidden behind the grass overhanging the edge of the wall. The first we knew of it was a loud snort and the sound of rocks being kicked about, and a rhino disappeared to my right. We froze. I looked down into the gulley, trying to see where the rhino was. There was nothing in sight as we were behind a slight bend. I was not too concerned, as the sides where we were would have challenged a baboon to climb, and the gulley was at least twenty feet deep. Silence. I motioned for the others to walk behind me, and we started forward as quietly as we could.

Suddenly, scarcely fifty feet in front of me, the front horn of a rhino appeared, followed by the wide-eyed head and flared ears of the owner! I half crouched in a flash, and the others froze too. The rhino appeared in front of us, paused with its head up, peering around, and then wandered away from us, tail curled over its departing rump. I breathed and looked back at my companions; they smiled nervously back. Two oxpeckers flew overhead and immediately called the alarm as they saw us. The rhino paused and turned around. The oxpeckers swooped down on to the rhino's back and immediately scuttled over to the other side of the animals back, just their heads and red bills showed over the prominent ridge of the backbone as they cussed us. We froze again. The rhino was now oblique to us and the wind direction. It was still close, now about thirty yards away, and standing head up, ears flared forward, looking back towards us.

He stared. We stared. None of us breathed. His ears switched backwards and forwards independently, testing. Nose raised, eyes blearily searching, still the oxpeckers cussed us. Eventually he turned and stalked off stiffly, rounded rump in armoured skin, tail curled into the distance and a peaceful morning.

We cautiously watched him disappear for a minute, and then I motioned for them to wait. I went down the side of the gulley, clutching at every little handhold, rifle, and pack over my shoulders. I scanned the gulley for anything large and then checked behind the bend, nothing there. I walked up where the rhino had exited in front of us and called my companions. We carried on and crossed up the wall on the other side. Talking in whispers and laughing nervously, we carried on, keeping a weather eye out for more rhino. We did see another one, but it was a long way off and lying in the shade of a *Terminalia,* enjoying a rest in the heat of the morning.

On another occasion, I was again up in the Matusadona and leading a walk for a group of men, and we had enjoyed a fun four days together. Chris Sewell was a good friend of mine, and he used to invite individuals from our local church to participate in a few days away as a time to share the Word and enjoy the bush. I had led several of them, and they were always really good fun.

In this instance, we were starting to descend from somewhere along the escarpment ridge and proceeding along a spur, with almost a steep slope on one side and a gentle scarp slope on the other. As we ambled along, the group were chatting quietly, and I was in the lead as usual. I suddenly heard the soft bickering of oxpeckers coming from ahead of me. I stopped. The group gradually ambled to a halt, talking softly. I motioned 'Quiet'. The oxpeckers carried on softly twittering, and I got a 'fix' on the noise. It was coming from a patch of tall grass not forty yards from us, right in our pathway. The wind was across us but quite fickle up here on the ridge, where it swirled and changed like flames in a wind. I quickly motioned for everybody to follow me, to the edge of the ridge, even though the wind was across our front. We paused, and I explained that there was 'something', probably a rhino in the grass just in front of us.

'Well, we want to see a rhino,' the group said, expectantly smiling at me.

'OK, so let's do it like this,' I responded. 'You all stay here on the edge of the trail, and let's see if we can get a view of it from here.'

'I'm assuming it's a rhino asleep. Just stay out of sight, that's all. If it does come out, it will likely head downhill anyway,' I said confidently, taking my pack off and hiding it behind a bush. The group moved to the edge of the ridge and started taking their packs off and getting cameras out. The birds spotted my movement and flew up, making their '*shreee, shree . . .*' alarm call. The grass moved, and a huge cow rhino stood up and walked out of cover, followed immediately by a tiny baby! I stood rock still and hoped the rest of the group were doing the same. She stared up the hill, eyes blinking and uncertain. The baby stood against the cow's legs, shy and unsteady, his nose with a tiny bump on it. Her ears flicked back and forth. She took a few more steps towards me and snorted . . . The birds had settled on a tree and were hysterical. Behind me, I could hear camera shutters and then the cow snorted again – the long, drawn-out raspberry. I backed off slowly and raised my hand to indicate 'Stop the cameras'.

I backed slowly, my boots crunching the gravel, and she became tense. She turned suddenly and trotted off with slow, bouncing strides a few yards down the trail, the little chap in her shadow. She paused to let the baby catch up and walked away, tail in the air – so huge, so protective, and so dangerous!

I watched her cautiously as her huge grey form vanished in the scrub Miombo that lined the edge of the trail. I drew a deep breath and looked at my happy crew, all had cameras poised and were watching where she had gone. 'Is that it?' They sounded disappointed. 'Yes, thank goodness. She was huge. Did you see the baby as well?' Lots of smiles and comments about how big she had looked and how big her horn was. We were lucky that her baby was so small; otherwise, she might have given us a run for our money!

We did not see another rhino on that walk, even though we had searched diligently along the slopes and trails. There was still a lot of spoor around and some middens had fresh dung in them. Their huge forms were often seen ambling along the game trails that wound up along the hillsides or feeding quietly on the *Diplorhyncus* or *Diospyros* bushes scattered through the woodland. They would like to lie on the point of ridges facing the lake. I think it was the cooling breeze that they enjoyed as they certainly would not have been able to enjoy the view as high as they were! The mountains were about 1,200 feet asl.

Rhino were not a problem on trail, but they were certainly a concern to me. My biggest 'fear' all those years ago when I was leading trails was the thought of being gored by a rhino through the lower abdomen, whilst carrying a pack on my back. It was a horrible thought so I was very careful, particularly going uphill on the trails as all sorts of animals, particularly rhino, used these trails all the time, and a rhino would merely charge downhill if they were disturbed and run straight over me!

RHINO ON THE NYAMUNI

One night, whilst camping on the Nyamuni River in the Matusadona, I had an interesting brush with a rhino which refused to be put off by my scent. I was leading a group of female friends, Patrick my brother-in-law and my wife, Gael on her first (and last trail).It was pitch-dark and about eight thirty, and we had all gone to bed. The area I had chosen was on a large termite mound with a flat top, big enough for seven of us to lie comfortably without touching, and I had scattered branches from a nearby dead tree around the periphery as a simple barrier. I was just settling into that comfortable pre-slumber, thankful that I had taken a moment to scrape a shallow 'hip-hole' in the hard surface of the earth. In the distance, lions called, and crickets punctuated the sound with shrill crickety noises. I smiled and listened to the shuffling sounds of my companions grow quiet as some of them recognised the lions' calls for what they were. Someone whispered.

Sleep blanketed me, and I drifted off. Squelchy, crunching noises woke me from close by. Alarmed, I focused on it . . . Damn, rhino, I thought, and very close. I sat up quickly, feeling for my flashlight and rifle, both items shared my narrow 'bed'. I listened a moment longer, reluctant to get out of my bed. Quickly slipping my shoes on, and dressed only in briefs, I rolled out of my bivvy and turned on the flashlight. There was a rhino feeding on the *Diospyros* bushes twelve feet from me. It turned and bolted into the dark, snorting and crashing away over trees and stumps for some distance. Dust waved and eddied in the beam of the light. Silence.

'We were wondering when you were going to wake up,' a voice from the dark said, 'What was it?'

'Rhino', I returned, 'and he was feeding on the Crocodile bark bushes here. He was really close, but I think he got a real fright when I put the light on him.' Everybody was awake now, talking quietly. 'Don't worry, it's unlikely he will be back,' I tried to sound reassuring as some of the group were visibly disturbed by sleeping out with 'wildlife'. I settled in carefully, tucking my net under my plastic groundsheet. I did not like sharing my bed with 'things' I couldn't see at night. Lying down took a certain amount of organisation, as one had to shuffle feet first down enough in the sleeping bag, then tuck the net in and then shuffle further until you were in completely. Then I made sure my rifle and flashlight were to hand, just in case.

Lying there wide awake, I listened for a while and then started to drift off. Fruit bats squeaked and honked in the Jackalberry trees by the river; all was quiet.

I heard a crack of a branch off my right. It just penetrated my sleep. I listened. Nothing moved. 'Could be elephant,' I thought. Relaxing now, I was about to let it wash over me, when a rhino snorted the 'raspberry' snort, long and drawn-out, a warning. I sprung up, rolled quickly out of bed, and sweeping up my rifle and light, switched it on and cast about. There was the rhino about twenty yards away, very alert and head-up. It charged off to one side, huffing and snorting, scattering branches and sticks, scaring everyone half out of their bags. I shouted at it and waved the light about to add effect; the shadows danced and gyrated like wild things. The rhino carried on huffing and puffing off through the thickets, diagonally towards the river, and I heard it splash noisily through.

'What are you doing, Gavin?' asked the anguished voices from the group of semi-recumbent bodies and mosquito nets hanging all awry, jiggling and swaying with agitation. I watched the commotion and felt uncontrollable laughter bubbling up. However, I stifled it with an effort and explained that the rhino had come back, so I had chased him away. I started to giggle and was immediately rebuked. 'What is SO damn funny? We are lying here, in the open, with lions and rhinos running around, and you laugh!' By now I was almost helpless with mirth. 'Yes, I know, but you didn't see your mosquito nets just now, dancing around like demented spooks on a wire!' Eventually, order was restored and shattered nerves calmed. It was now about midnight and getting chilly, so after considerable muted chatter and shuffling around of sleeping bags and rearranging of nets, quiet descended on to the camp. I had slipped back into my bag quite quickly and was still shaken by the giggles every now and then as the memory of it all came back to me.

Well, at about half past one, the rhino returned! He had come across the river and walked his way towards the camp, feeding noisily again on twigs and leaves again. The twigs crackled like cornflakes in his great mouth, between huge molars, and he slurped and squelched noisily as he ate. I could not believe it. I was awake in a nano second and rolled out of my bag before my eyes had focused properly. I silently and with a dimmed light cupped in my hand, walked towards the noise behind the dark bole of a Jackalberry, and then let a beam of light probe across the small clearing from where we were. There, in the light, was a rhino munching contentedly on a crocodile bark, his back to me. His rounded black shadow was projected on to the bushes. I stared at him and wondered what I should do. I thought about the group slumbering (I hoped) behind me and knew that it would be too much for one or two of them to get out of 'bed' quietly and quickly to see this fellow. 'Damn it,' I thought, 'let me do it.' So I pottered back and, as quietly as I could, woke them and told them in whispers that I had another rhino in view. Two of them immediately slid out of bed and joined me; the others were undecided. I left them then, and we snuck back to look at my prize. I let a narrow beam of light out towards the sound, and for a few seconds, he was still, his eyes half closed and relaxed. 'Wow, he's HUGE,' said a whispered voice behind me. There was more noise behind me from the camp, and someone turned on a light which flickered through the nets and lit them up for a bout ten seconds. That was it. The rhino stopped eating, turned nimbly around, stared at the light, and snorted a 'raspberry' snort, taking a few steps towards us, as we were in a direct line between him and the camp. The light went out, but the rhino didn't! I stood in shock for a moment and then he saw my light cupped in my hand and charged.

All I could see was a rhino coming, and so I bellowed. I also dropped the light, as I swung my rifle around to fire into the ground. The rhino skidded to a halt and thundered off into the night. My flashlight bounced and rolled a bit, adding to the effect in the swirling dust and mayhem. The two behind me had vanished with squeaks, leaving a pair of slops (sandals) behind, and there was a scream followed by several screams from the camp. I snatched the light up and followed the rhino for a few yards, just to see where it had gone, the sound of its retreat quite loud and obvious.

Then I made my way back to the camp, which, by then, had several lights flashing around it, like a mini traffic centre. 'OK, are you all all right?' I asked loudly as there was an awful lot of noise going on. I deposited the sandals. 'Oh that's where they are!' The owner collected them and put them on. 'Where did I leave them?'

'Hanging in mid-air when you bolted,' I smiled.

'What happened, was it a rhino or a lion?'

'How many were there?'

'A lion . . . ? I thought you said it was rhino!' Indignant.

' OK, calm down, it was just another rhino, OK? He obviously favours this patch, and we happened to be in the middle of it. Now, everybody just relax and calm down. I think he's gone a long way away.'

'How do you know? You said that last time . . .'

'Bloody hell, aNother friggin' rhino! I thought they were rare?'

'I am NOT going to sleep again. I can't stand it. My nerves are shot from all this . . .'

'Did you see him?' Awestruck wonder. 'Yes, he was HUGE! And so happy just munching away, until somebody turned the light on him. Shame, you gave him such a fright!' Indignant sandal-owner again. Giggles broke out amongst the group and then loud laughter, including mine. We laughed until we nearly cried, and then relived the whole experience again, each giving their own version. What a laugh!

It was useless trying to get to sleep, so I made a pot of tea and shared it with half the group, and then made another pot. I gave up trying to sleep that night just in case the fellow came back yet again!

Another funny story involved a honeymoon couple who were from the great United States of America. He was about six foot eight, and she was about five foot five! He was a trails leader for some trekking company and had a custom-made backpack for his huge frame. They were a delightful couple and never complained about anything, just marched along, enjoying it all.

Dave Christensen was serving time with me as an apprentice guide then, and he was with me on this trip. (Dave is a highly sought-after guide to this day and works largely in Tanzania now.)

We had walked for several days with this couple and seen all manner of great things but no rhino. We had bathed in tiny streams, drunk water from my secret springs at the base of the escarpment, enjoyed fabulous sunsets from the top of the escarpment and stalked elephants, lions, and buffalo apart from learning how to cook blueberry pie on the trail. (The American trail guide had introduced us to this amazing pre-packed and easy-to-cook-delicacy!) That was my first blueberry pie, truly an American icon.

Towards the end of our trip, we were traversing a steep-sided game trail along the edge of a stream and heading down into a thicket at the base of the hills. Suddenly, there on the path, facing us was a rhino, lying down half asleep.

We stopped literally in mid stride and gazed down at this wonderful beast, lying there in the middle of the path, a mere thirty feet away. Silently we backed off, on tiptoe, and only when we were a way down the track did we stop and congratulate ourselves on this remarkable find. 'A Black rhino, asleep in front of us . . . Can you believe it!' Such jubilation. Dave and I smiled hugely at each other. 'OK, we will drop our packs behind these rocks just in case he rushes for us and finds them. Unlikely, seeing as it is up a hill, but you never know with these fellows,' I cautioned. They looked aghast. 'What? Do you mean he would destroy our packs? Well, I'm going to keep mine on,' was the man's answer. 'Well, you won't be able to move quickly with the pack on and that rhino might just explode into action at any moment,' I said earnestly, lodging my pack out of sight in the rocks off the trail. He reluctantly unstrapped his Bergen and moved it way off the trail high up in a cleft in the rocks where even a honey badger would have struggled to reach it.

That settled, we mentioned cameras. 'Oh dear,' he said. He went clambering back and rescued his pack, retrieved his camera, zipped the pack up again, and laboriously re-hid the pack. By now, I was getting twitchy and was certain the rhino would have gone off without us knowing, so we silently walked back to our vantage point. The rhino was still there, fast asleep. I motioned to the husband to take a picture . . . just one. We waited with baited breath . . . He focused and we waited. No, he hadn't wound it on. (Some film cameras in those days had to be wound on after taking a picture.) Quietly, he wound it on, focused again, and 'click', took a picture. We waited crouched behind cover. The rhino's ears stirred, flopped forward and backwards. His breath made little swirls in the dust in front of each nostril. His one front leg was bent at the knee, half raised and the other was tucked underneath him as he lay in the shade on the trail. He sighed, creating bigger swirls. I motioned to the husband again, take another one. Click. The rhino slumbered on. We looked at each other in disbelief. We were scarcely forty feet away, and this rhino was sleeping . . . still.

Take another photo, I signalled. He motioned 'no', he didn't want a picture of a sleeping rhino. 'Huh, he's lucky to see a rhino', I thought. Dave and I conferred quietly and crawled back to the waiting couple. 'We are going to try and call him to us.' Unethical really, but effective normally. I assured them, 'Dave is a master at this.' We repositioned ourselves, choosing our escape trees with care. Dave 'called'. Silence . . . again, again . . . the dust swirled around his nostrils, the ears waggled . . . The rhino talk went out again, hanging in the air like an intrusion. The ears waggled again and then it registered. The rhino lifted its great horned head and stared up the hill towards our hiding place. Dave called . . . The rhino stared a moment longer and then dropped his pointed lip into the trail and closed his eyes, giving a great sigh as he did so! We stared and looked at each other, suppressing the desire to laugh. I looked back at the couple and made a helpless gesture with my hands. They stared at me and then at the rhino again.

We crawled out of our hiding spot and went back to them. 'You know what, we can't disturb this fellow any more, so we are going to leave him be. It is unheard of for a rhino to be this relaxed up here, so we will go around him, OK?' I whispered to them. They readily agreed and so we collected our gear and gathered back on the trail up the hill a short distance.

Naturally, they wanted to know more about this rhino and so I explained what he was doing and something about their habits too.

'This is the most relaxed rhino I think I have ever seen!' I said and so we left quietly walking back up the trail a short way before finding a different route down to another of my secret springs at the base of the hill.

There we made tea and had breakfast. They were disappointed. 'We thought rhino were supposed to be all fired up and aggressive when disturbed.'

'Well, they can be,' Dave answered, 'but this chap has obviously had a long night and is knackered. They don't normally behave like that.'

I hope that rhino had a good long and undisturbed day, he needed it!

Within the next two years, we lost nearly all our rhino to poachers from Zambia and Zimbabwe, and the 'Rhino Wars' took part of Africa's great wildlife heritage away, driven by an insatiable Middle Eastern and Asian market. One day, I hope Zimbabwe's story will be told by one more skilled than I, of the brave men and women who fought a very real war against a tyranny of men, both within the country's government and from the neighbouring countries.

Now only their ghosts haunt these mountains and valleys of the Zambezi.

*As I write this now, South Africa is in the midst of the slaughter, and the insidious tentacles of greed have tainted every facet of society. Still it goes on.

ELEPHANTS ON TRAIL

Elephants are amazing animals, and even though I have seen thousands of these 'long-nosed lumberjacks' over the years, I am still impressed by them as a species and all of their abilities.

During the years on the trails, I had several really interesting encounters with them.

Mana Pools National Park is a World Heritage Site in northern Zimbabwe, on the Zambezi River, where Zambia's Lower Zambezi National Park is on the opposite bank. Animals cross regularly from one side to the other in safety and, in particular, elephants. Quite often, during my trails down to Chikwenya from Nyamepi, we would watch breeding herds or small groups of bulls crossing the river or just to islands in the river to feed on the stands of *Phragmites* reeds or *Panicum* grass. It was always fun to watch youngsters holding on to their mothers' tail as they got deeper and deeper until they had to swim. Baby elephants swim very well, with strong 'doggy paddle', and whilst the herd was swimming or wading, the little ones would be paddling away between the group. Naturally, there were disasters when babies would be separated from their siblings or mother and be swept away to drown or die alone way downstream. We did find drowned babies infrequently whilst canoeing down the river. When the herds emerged from the water, they would be black and shiny, with clean white ivory, or they would have a water mark at some point on their hides, which made for an interesting photograph if one was able to get close enough without disturbing them.

I would try and give my trailists good sightings of any wildlife, and elephants were always approachable, provided the wind was right and we had good cover. Once I had been surprised by a big bull whilst crossing a wide open area, deeply pitted by big foot prints during the dry season. The result was it was a difficult surface to hurry across because it was so broken and we were all laden with heavy packs. So, we had nowhere to hide, so to speak. He came out of the woodland thinking deep elephantine thoughts and totally unaware that strangers were nearby. I stopped the group and stood still, telling everybody to keep still as he had not seen us and would get a fright when he did. He was about sixty yards away and going to cross diagonally in front of us, and we were in a little depression, so he had a slight height advantage. The chances were that he was going to be startled and then trumpet at us, so I whispered to my group to stand fast. When he was about forty yards away, I spoke gently to him, telling him that I apologised for spoiling his day, but I would take my group away, and he could carry on. He jerked to a halt and turned to scurry away, tail up and ears flapping.

Then he stopped and turned around . . . paused, lifted his head, and stared down his tusks at us. His head was raised, and he was tense. I waited for it . . . He stared and then made a rush for us. Just a few yards and stopped and gave us a screaming blast through his trunk! Some of my group jumped. 'Stand still,' I said, 'and you . . . (to the elephant) are scaring everybody. I have apologised, now please push off.' The bull's tail was still stiff with tension and standing out sideways. He stared down his tusks at us, his coffee-brown eyes wide with fear and anger. It was touch-and-go. I stood, rifle in one hand, ready to shout if he charged us again and wave my arms about, or if he changed his mind, to shoot him. I suppose it was just a matter of seconds, but it seemed a while longer before he shook his head and stiffly turned away, still standing tall and walked off at an angle, still watching us from one eye. We remained still, although I could feel the tension drain from my group with each dusty step he took away from us. 'Phew,' someone said, 'they are impressive when they are on foot!'

I answered, 'They certainly are, and sometimes they are calm and at other times they want to kill you, just because way back, they had a bad experience with another human somewhere, or they are just feeling grumpy!' We watched the bull walk towards and into a grove of fever-berry crotons, his bulk disappearing in seconds behind the fresh green of the leaves, and out of sight. 'OK, let's go,' I said conversationally, and we carried on.

Behind me, there was silence as my group gathered themselves and breathed. 'I need a loo-stop,' one of the women said rather plaintively and so headed towards the nearest cover which was still forty metres or so away.

Generally, elephants were never a problem, and provided one took care about avoiding thick cover on hot days and being careful which way the wind was going to carry one's scent with breeding herds about, they were safe to be with.

Naturally, not everyone was that lucky. There was a civilian lecturer from the university who walked into the jesse once and was mortally injured by a cow herd of elephant. He had survived the initial attack it seemed and managed to drag himself into some trees, only to die sometime during the night before the rangers found his battered body the next day. A young woman had been fearfully gored by a buffalo many years before whilst visiting Mana on her honeymoon. She died almost immediately, a huge tragedy.

Several guides had had to shoot elephants on different occasions in spite of great care being taken whilst on walks to avoid such incidents. One elephant cow had charged a guide from 114 paces, after first picking up his scent from behind some trees and coming straight at the group. He had run his group up a tall termite mound to hide them, and the cow had followed him so that he had almost touched her ear with the barrel of his rifle as he shot her! That was close. It says a lot about their eyesight and sense of smell that she was able to zero in on him from such a distance and push home her attack.

There are several other cases too, and it seemed that as the dry season progressed, the cow herds became more stressed and were more touchy. So September and October (the hottest months before the rains) were the worst, and we all tiptoed around the breeding herds, giving them a wide berth.

PAINTED DOGS, UNIQUE PREDATORS

These wonderful and maligned animals have in recent decades become known for the fact that they are endangered in Africa. In the early post-WWII years, when the 'Bambi syndrome' prevailed, predators as a whole were destroyed by game managers at every opportunity. Even in national parks, in the very early days, they were poisoned and shot, the dens blocked up, and adults had a bounty placed on their heads or tails!

Thankfully, conservation biologists have seen the sun, and this is a thing of the distant past in parks. However, there are still misguided individuals who persist in shooting them on private land in the mistaken belief that they destroy the game, instead of realising that the dogs function as 'movers and shakers' of antelope populations and keep the herds free of 'imperfect' sick or lame individuals.

In recent years, ecotourists have come to regard the dogs as a form of trophy, to be added to their list of the Big Five, which has two edges to it. It creates a demand on the guides to find dogs and therefore increases the disturbance of their dens and lives, but at the same time, it is a marvellous opportunity to educate travellers to the real plight of these amazing predators. They are always interesting animals to watch, and particularly, when they start waking up for the afternoon hunt.

Typically Painted Dogs hunt in the morning and then in the afternoon, during the cooler parts of the daytime hours. They are at risk at night as they do not have a cat's nocturnal vision, and lion do kill them frequently when they are on the move after dark. The social structure of the pack is quite simply this. There is an 'alpha male' and an 'alpha female' who dominate the other individuals in the pack. Only they are allowed to breed, and the whole pack assists with keeping the pups fed (after weaning) and babysitting the pups at the den when they are still too small to move. Young females leave the pack when the numbers reach a threshold of sustainable-food availability and some males may leave too. They require vast areas of land over which to range and invariably come into contact with village dogs somewhere during their rambles. Most village dogs have never been inoculated against rabies, canine distemper, canine flu, and various other common but fatal diseases. The mortality amongst populations of Painted dogs is very high in the vicinity of any settlements, and although disease is a major contributor, there are others. Poisoning due to the fear over livestock predation, dens being blocked, pups killed, and totally unnecessary shootings by hunters are other reasons for deaths.

They have no 'road sense' either, and road-kills are high where trucks are travelling at night or just through wildlife areas. Truckers are generally unsympathetic to wildlife on the roads in many places in the world!

Several researchers have established themselves in Southern Africa, namely in Zimbabwe, Zambia, and Botswana where they have been welcomed and continue to contribute to scientific understanding of *Lycaon pictus*, the 'Painted Wolf'.

In the early hours of the morning, the pack will start to wake up. Certain individuals will get up, shake themselves, and lie down, dozing a little, waiting for the sun to warm them. Other members of the pack may rise, stretch, and shake and then suddenly run from one to another, uttering whiny-chittering sounds. This precipitates a frenzy of greeting ceremonies amongst the pack with much defecating and licking of muzzles by lower-ranking dogs. Once every member of the pack is participating in this ceremony, one dog will decide to take the lead, and they will suddenly file off into the bush to find food.

On sighting an antelope suitable for the kill, the leaders will immediately break into a sprint and run the animal down. The pack will spread out within an area, and it is a rather loosely co-ordinated hunt, as pack members will become separated from each other. If one of the members catch and kill an antelope, they will not call and announce it, but the fellow pack members seem to have an uncanny instinct about this and will often come running in and share in the spoils. In a pack with large pups, the pups are allowed to eat first, followed by the two alpha animals and finally the rest of the pack. This hierarchical system is unique amongst terrestrial predators and truly astonishing to witness.

I have only witnessed this in Botswana and Zimbabwe, and so would be interested to receive any observations on this behaviour from other persons with similar experiences.

After eating, the pack sleeps and relaxes, and in the afternoon again, it will invariably hunt again to satisfy those individuals who did not eat much in the morning.

There are no valid recorded cases of Painted Dogs attacking humans. It is possible to sit quietly on the ground with a sleeping pack and enjoy being in the close proximity of these animals and share some of their most peaceful moments!

I have often encountered a pack on walks in different areas of Zimbabwe and sat quietly with my guests within a few metres of the animals which, after an initial curiosity and alarm, calm down and lie down in scattered groups amongst the grass and leaf-litter.

The first time I encountered 'dogs' on a walk was in Hwange, when I was doing a walk from the Safari lodge there with a mixed group of guests from the lodge. We had had a wonderful few hours walking through the teak and had just arrived at Kanondo Pan (this was long before the lodge was built there) and were just enjoying the ambience and looking at spoor in the mud around the pan. Suddenly, I spotted a shadowy form watching us quietly from the shadows of the teak. It was a single dog. I quietly told everybody about it, and there was a frisson of panic amongst them. 'We're going to be eaten alive . . . Oh my, what are we going to do? . . . Shoot it quickly before it tells all the others we are here!' There was a sudden shift of moods from one of nervous bonhomie at having had a great walk through the 'African bush' to terror. It amazed and shocked me.

'Whoa,' I said, 'we have nothing to fear . . . it's only a Painted dog?' Puzzled, I frowned at everyone. 'It is not going to bother us. Come, let's go and say hello,' I tried to calm them. 'NO . . . We can't do that, it may not be alone.' This came from a young woman dressed in sky blue pants and pale top. 'They won't harm us, I promise you that,' I said to her, taking her by the hand.

The group gathered behind me as I slowly walked at a slight angle towards the animal, which stood calmly watching our approach. Ears pricked, it allowed us to get within about a hundred feet of it when it gave a guttural growl-bark and disappeared into the teak.

There was an unnatural quiet from everybody behind me, and I carried on. alone, except for the young woman I had firmly by the hand. I turned around. 'Come on, you lot, follow me please!' They were hesitant, and dropped back, nervous and twittering like a flock of guineafowl. I was not going to convince them, so I sat down where I was in the open. The group joined me, sitting close to each other, expectant. 'The dogs won't harm us, I can tell you now. They may come out and approach us if we sit quietly and then get our scent, study us curiously, and then wander off. It will be amazing!' I smiled reassuringly at my unhappy group. They smiled nervously, fidgeted and talked quietly. After a few minutes, six 'dogs' emerged from the woodland and stopped. Staring at us. They growled and then walked forward a few steps. My group stared, horrified . . . in fact, looking a little like terrified impala, all big eyes and nerves! One woman closed her eyes and put her hands over her face. I was alarmed at the obvious fear they all had of these wonderful animals. I waited and the dogs sat down on their haunches, looking at us. I started to describe their social life and how two individuals lead the pack, when more dogs emerged at a run from the woodland on the other side of us. Two stopped and growled, but the other three, youngsters, carried on gambolling and almost ran into us! They leapt into the air, giving their funny little growly bark and dashed off to the first group, looking back at us. By now, my group had ceased to breathe and sweaty faces stared out.

I couldn't help it. I started to giggle. My group looked at me with complete helplessness, a little miffed I think. 'See,' I said, 'they won't hurt us. They are just curious and have probably never seen humans like us before. Think of what we smell like – all the deodorants and body odours we are giving off.' I had to laugh again and some of them did too. The pack now walked towards us, stopping and testing the air a mere a few yards from us, their yellow eyes wary and bright. 'Move slowly and take a picture,' I whispered. The dogs started to back off a little but watched us minutely. They were beautiful. Their lean, almost skinny bodies tightly filled with a recent meal, and some of their ruffs stiff with blood from a kill. Their yellow-black-and–white blotch-patterned coats blending with each other, the huge dark round ears stark above their watchful yellow eyes.

Suddenly, the alpha dog turned and walked away from us, his ears less tense and his attitude relaxed. He wandered off to the shade and lay down, stretching out, enjoying the shade and cool grass. The rest of the pack followed his example except for the young dogs who stared at us, still wary but not frightened.

My group meanwhile had calmed down a little and were staring interestedly at the animals, whispering amongst themselves. I explained the difference in the sexes and some of their biology, all the while sitting quietly in the sun. 'Oh, they look just like dogs . . . ,' disappointment sounded in their voice. I explained that they were all carnivores, but these were not like domestic dogs; they were, in fact, a form of 'Wild dog', and that wild dogs were found elsewhere in the world too. 'I thought they were dogs gone wild,' she smiled sweetly, 'but these are lovely. A bit skinny, mind you, but so pretty. What is that stuff under their throats . . . in the hair?' 'Dried blood,' I answered. She looked horrified. 'Why. What happened to it?' 'They kill antelope for food, you know. Impala, kudu, young wildebeest, and zebra sometimes.' I stared at her curiously. She paled visibly and clutched her face in her hands. 'So we are in danger!' I paused, took a deep breath. 'Absolutely not . . . They don't chase or eat people. You don't look like an impala or anything they are familiar with eating or smell or behave like a prey item. So stop worrying, please.' We sat there a little while longer and then, when all the dogs were lying quietly and most were dozing off, with one or two still watching us through half-closed eyes, I motioned for the group to move off. We 'crabbed' away sideways on our hands and feet so that we would not disturb the dogs, which by now were quite relaxed with us, and although a few raised their heads as we started moving, none of them took fright and ran away.

Since then, it has become quite common for guides to sit with 'dogs' and enjoy them. It is one of the greatest thrills to be intimate with this predator.

Painted dogs are to be found in healthy numbers in northern Botswana, Zimbabwe, and to some level in South Africa too. Kenya and Tanzania have smaller populations (it would seem), but these are often outside the access of most tourists in either private ranch conservancies or community concessions. On a recent trip through those countries, the guides reported seeing them in small numbers on the border between Kenya and Tanzania around the Kogatende section.

SOME BABOONS DO EAT MEAT

I have seen baboons (both Chacma and Olive) chase and catch young antelope and devour the meat with relish. I also photographed a male yellow baboon which had leapt up and caught a spur-winged goose in flight and eaten it! The same animal had apparently been seen the previous week with another bird, so he had learnt to do this and was now benefiting from a new skill.

Generally, baboons feed on a wide range of items, both vegetable and 'animal', being primarily various arthropods and lizards too.

New-born impala, bushbuck, gazelles, red lechwe, adult and young scrub hares, guineafowl and their chicks, and other ground-nesting birds are all potential prey for adult baboons.

I was conducting a walk one morning at Xigera, a lovely camp in the Okavango Delta, Botswana, when we chanced upon a group of baboons acting strangely. (Actually, we had paused briefly in our walk to teach my American guests how to play cricket, using a palm tree as wickets, palm nuts as a ball, and a suitable stick for a bat.) Elephants fed calmly in the distance, baboons and monkeys foraged in the bush close by, and Red lechwe grazed in the shallows of a flood plain. It was a lovely morning.

A small group of impala had galloped snorting past us before we had stopped, and after checking to see what had caused their flight and seeing nothing, I had dismissed it and started playing. I then noticed a group of adult male and female baboons sidling over to a clump of taller grass, and watching the area intently. They sat, almost nonchalantly, at various points of high ground in full view of the grass island, keeping a close eye on it. I called a halt to our game and collecting my rifle, approached the grass, with my guests behind me.

The baboons allowed me to come very close to them, so fixed in interest were they. I walked into the grass following a game trail, even though the grass was bent over the pathway, hiding it. Suddenly a male baboon ran out, his muzzle covered in fresh blood. The other baboons stared at him. So did we!

He walked away reluctantly and sat a short distance from us, wiping his muzzle with his hands. I walked further in and found a yearling impala, dead and partially disembowelled.

The impala was a female, and her liver had been removed, and the top of her head bitten open, exposing the brain which was partially eaten! Everybody was a bit shocked at this murderous act by what they considered a humorous and benevolent ape, so I had to explain it all. After explaining the scene to everybody, we left the carcase and returned to our cricket tree, to collect our belongings, and finished our walk. Baboons are often associated with impala because the baboons drop fresh leaves and fruit from trees, which the impala, feeding below, rapidly and gratefully eat. At lambing time, impala ewes are sometimes more careful about their simian associates and keep their babies away from baboon troops. Even threatening individual baboons with lowered heads if they come too close to them and their young ones.

I have seen olive baboons chase and catch newborn Thomson's gazelles in the Mara, whilst the mothers' frantic and heroic efforts to protect their babies often fail, and the baboons easily carry off the lambs and then dismember and eat them. However, it is not all baboons that do this, and I believe it is a learned behaviour that only a small percentage of male baboons exhibit. I have not seen a female baboon (either chacma, olive, or yellow) initiate a chase ever, although they willingly solicit meat from the males involved.

I was on a safari in the beautiful Luangwa Valley a few years ago and was present when a yellow baboon caught and ate a spur-winged goose. We had stopped for lunch at a lagoon somewhere in the woodlands there and were quietly enjoying the peace and tranquillity of the area. A small flock of spur-winged geese flew low over the weed-covered water, moving away from us to a point further along the lagoon. As the birds flew over a section of the lagoon where some baboons were foraging, a large immature male leapt into the air and caught a goose! He quickly subdued and killed the struggling bird and calmly started to eat the breast. I was totally astonished.

Gathering my guests into the vehicle, we drove slowly up the lagoon until we were opposite the scene and watched the process from there. I managed to collect a number of images, despite the distance between us and the kill. He ate at least half the breast, before pausing. Two other baboons sat nearby watching him. The one female sat and watched him closely, and when he moved off, she immediately went forward and ate sparingly off the carcase, leaving her mouth bloody. At this point, two tawny eagles flew down, followed by a white-headed vulture, and the baboon moved off. I photographed the two eagles having a tussle in mid-air. The third baboon then investigated the carcase and also fed off it.

An amazing and interesting incident.

MANA POOLS – THE EARLY DAYS OF ADVENTURE

Mana Pools is such a wonderful part of the Zambezi valley and features commonly in my career.

I used to guide tented safaris for a friend in this beautiful park and was privileged to be one of the first guides to operate there too.

Daily early-morning walks, canoeing the Zambezi, and game drives were all part of my life.

The floodplain has always been a special place. Here one could count up to thirteen different species of mammal, simultaneously from one spot, particularly in the dry autumnal months. Various cameos from my visits come to mind with clarity: walking across the plains in the mornings, with soft rays of the sun highlighting the baboons sitting in the sun on the termite mounds; the dust hanging in the crisp, golden air disturbed by the sharp but dainty hooves of the herds of impala as they feed on the fallen flowers of the sausage trees; tree squirrels huddling together, four deep on an exposed branch, their tails fluffed out and clutching each other for warmth and security, shiny dark eye's slightly glazed as they feel the warmth of the weak winter sun filtering through the branches and sparse leaves of the Acacias; hornbills and Burchell's starlings foraging on the ground, flicking the small, dark piles of freshly turned soil and picking up harvester termites; and the hornbills tossing them back into their open throats, uttering little satisfied throaty calls. Beautiful memories to share.

In the early 1980s, canoeing safaris started. There was always a sense of excitement when we pushed off into the current on those mornings – the water was invariably warmer than the air, the light was clear, no wind, and the current would nudge us along as we just enjoyed the river as it was. Life was good.

The typical trip meant that we would start at either Kariba, actually 5 km downstream of the wall, Chirundu or Mana Pools itself for the final stretch of the river to Kanyemba.

Night-stops would be on designated islands, mosquito nets would act as tents, meals would be cooked by the guide on a fire (later, it had to be a gas cooker), very little alcohol was carried on trips, except for wine and a few beers. Zimbabwean wine was in its infancy – always a journey of bottled uncertainty.

There had been a serious incident with a lion attacking a female guest on a commercial safari, and since then, National Parks had allowed canoe trips to camp over-night on certain islands to reduce the risk of predator attack. Troy Williamson, then a young Canoe Guide, with Canoeing Safaris had saved this girl's life by chasing the lion with his paddle, not once but twice in the same incident, as the lion returned for the girl later, having had a go at her earlier in the evening. She was in the middle of her monthly cycle, and this was thought to have caused the lion to have singled her out amongst the several people there. She was sleeping in the middle of the crowd, and he still grabbed her feet and sleeping-bag!

Interestingly enough, in all the years we operated there, no crocodile attacks were reported on sleeping guests at night stops. Although attacks on people, who were in the water for some reason or another, were recorded over the years, there was no direct land-based aggression. One crocodile took to climbing into canoes at a certain night spot, looking for food scraps, as it had become used to finding scraps left by canoeists over several weeks. Despite warning Parks about this animal, and asking canoeists not to feed this animal, it became a problem and was finally destroyed by a young canoe guide who decided enough was enough, and he shot it as it clambered into a canoe on the beach! Needless to say, he was smartly chastised by the local warden for his actions.

Those early canoe trips were filled with adventure and hard work too. When the wind blew, invariably it blew straight up-river creating waves nearly half a metre high, which gradually filled the canoes with water, causing them to wallow, roll over, and tip terrified people into the turbulent river. August and September could be really tiresome months. Strong winds would suddenly hit you, creating a major problem, and stinging sandstorms would compound the chaos. Hippo would submerge as well and increase the risk of collision with the canoes battling the heavy waves. There was little to be done except to pull over and wait for as long as possible before moving on to a safe pull-out point. People in the water would have to be rescued quickly as we all had a fear of crocodiles grabbing a guest or one of us.

Only in 2007 did the unthinkable happen. A canoe was attacked by a crocodile, and a young girl fell out and was taken by the crocodile. We all had incidents with crocodiles at some stage, but in 2007, a distinct increase in attacks was experienced. These were big crocodiles which would suddenly appear and deliberately and directly attack the canoes, biting them across the middle or the ends and start pushing them out into deep water. Fisher Ngwerume, a long-term canoe guide told me his story.

'It was a rainy day, and we were pushing (canoeing) slowly down the river. Suddenly a big croc appeared, bit my canoe in the middle, and started to swim towards the middle of the river. I tried to shout, but my voice failed. I beat the head with my paddle, very, very hard, and broke the paddle. My pistol (.44 mag.) was under the canvas, out of the rain. I hit the crocodile in the eyes with my broken paddle and his head pulled back . . . and as he started to sink again, his teeth hooked in the net, tipping the canoe over. I could see the pattern of his neck scales – they were worn smooth. He was an old crocodile. Suddenly, the net slipped off, and the croc was gone, and my canoe came upright again. I took the spare paddle and went to the bank. My legs were shaking, and my heart was full.'

While discussing the increasing number of croc attacks amongst the more experienced canoe guides, most agreed that it was a result of the apparently uncontrolled development along the Zambian bank and the vast increase in motor-boat traffic in the deep channel. Several incidents were recorded over this period, and many scary stories collected. Canoeing had changed, and a tinge of apprehension now floated along with every trip dipping paddles in the Lower Zambezi!

The big crocodiles were moving over to the far quieter side of the river, where game was still plentiful along the Mana Pool's river front, and so canoes were being presented to these big animals. Naturally, some have become very bold and started attacking the slow-moving, harmless canoes! Very unnerving!

Walking across the floodplain, beneath the 'albidas', was a treasure that we all loved to do and a great privilege. The early-morning walks tracked the activities of lions and leopard during the night or the measured spoor of elephant bulls that had been feeding on the seedpods of the thorn trees. Spotted hyenas too became a major scavenger over time, and their depredations into the campsite caused us all huge headaches. Most of us still have 'cooler boxes' with teeth marks in them, years after our last safaris there! They became bold enough to climb up on to the bonnets of our Land Rovers and steal the bags from inside the spare tyre.

Honey badgers were also characters that we had to deal with on an infrequent basis, day and night.

One sometimes encountered them either in the rank *Vitiveria* spp. grass or in the thickets. Normally, they would growl and then there would be a rushing sound through the grass . . . Needless to say, they certainly stimulated the blood pressure in seconds, as we could not always see what it was we were looking at as they are so short. None of us ever really got THAT close to them for them to be a danger to us, despite the lurid stories one hears. Elephants would be strolling about, feeding on the creepers or branches. Great bundles of leaves would be pulled down to mouth level and pushed in with the trunk, leaving a gentle confetti drift of green leaves around their forelegs.

In pod season, the cow herds would appear in numbers. Their herds would drift out of the jesse in quiet groups and head deliberately for long-remembered spots to scoop up the pods. Delicate clouds of dust would follow them, visited sporadically by darting drongos, hawking insects from the air behind the grey bodies. If one stood close to them, carefully down-wind and hidden in a jumble of branches, the rasp of skin on skin could be plainly heard, and the muted rumbles of 'elephant-talk' was far reaching. From October onwards, one had to be very careful when approaching these herds on foot, as the matriarchs were really stressed and sensitive to any humans. So we would avoid any unnecessary approaches in the hot, dry season.

One well-known guide was charged from over 114 paces by a cow (with a calf), who chased him up a termite hill, forcing him to shoot her in self-defence of himself and his clients. Another guide was charged from over 100 paces in similar circumstances and tried to hide from her by running quietly behind a line of trees and shrubs. She tracked his scent using her trunk, and he had to shoot her too.

After a 'self-defence shooting', we were required to submit a statement from ourselves and our guests, outlining the whole incident. This then was submitted to the warden for his assessment.

In all the years guides started walking in the parks, elephant and buffalo were the majority of the 'problem' animals. Rarely was a lioness shot, and never a lion! There was a marked difference between guiding/walking in a hunting area and a (non-hunting) National Park. Animals were relaxed and more 'approachable' than those in the hunting areas, where humans on foot are a danger to be avoided or charged. Simple.

Only two guides were ever killed or injured by animals, and no guests between 1980 and 2000. A tribute to the standards attained and maintained by the licensing authority and the association which set these originally.

One guide was killed by an elephant cow, when he was leading his first walk. He had been licensed by National Parks when he was an employee of the government and did not have the experience necessary, although he maintained he did. The proof was in the elephant-gored body the assistant guide had to bury in his sleeping bag under logs and rocks so that he, the assistant, could walk the traumatised clients out of the area back to the main road.

The second guide (actually a PH) was badly injured by trying to hide behind a termite mound from a musth elephant bull. The bull ran straight over the mound, knocking the guide unconscious, then chased and killed two of the three guests behind him. A tragedy that no one could have foreseen. Animals can never be totally trusted to do as they have been doing for long periods. I'm sure they have good days and off days, as we do. In fact, just by watching many animals, even those familiar to us on a daily basis, one can pick up small signs that should warn us when it's an off day!

Those days at Chikwenya when leading early-morning walks off across the Sapi floodplain into Mana were the happiest days I can remember. I remember one morning, going off from the camp as usual across the sandy river bed, several old buffalo bulls were also walking over, parallel to my group, but about 200 metres upstream. The group stopped, stared a moment, and then plodded on. One cranky old chap, with a wide spread and bloodshot eyes, stopped and turned his head as far as he could and watched us with a jaundiced eye. It was written all over his face! Trouble!

We would always give him a wide berth when setting off in the mornings, and his little group happened to be in the vicinity as well.

LET SLEEPING LIONS BE!

Tracking lions is always exciting. Even though we talk about it for a while, before actually doing it, guests always get really excited and apprehensive about going off into the bush. Even guides get excited. Interestingly, it would seem now (in 2015) that in many of the national parks that we work now, lions are becoming just a *little* used to seeing people on foot. This supposes that those same lions are being subjected to humans on foot regularly? Possibly.

In 1988, tracking lions in the Matusadona was a mission, as the lions would cover long distances nightly during a normal 'patrol' movement and were not used to being followed up by *Homo sapiens*! One particular incident comes to mind with lions.

I was guiding a small group camping in the Matusadona who were very active and interested. We were camped in the riverine forest of one of the rivers draining north out of the Matusadona National Park, quite away from the lake shore itself. They had spent two days in the camp, and we had tried hard to find lions for them, to no avail. Everything else had been relatively easy to locate, including a rhino, but although we could often hear lion roars at night, we had failed to track them to contact, owing primarily to the distance being just too much for our 'mature' guests having just not quite enough energy to walk for the hours needed!

Anyway, the days of the trip were limited, as they are, and so we set out an hour earlier than normal on our last morning, determined to find these wretched lions.

Driving to where I thought the lions had been calling, I cast about along the stream bed that traversed the gravel track and eventually located what I thought was spoor fresh enough to follow. After the normal pre-walk briefing, we set off in single file as the sun's rays were feeling their way through the topmost branches of the Jackalberry trees. The bird chorus had been in full swing for a while, and the air was crisp and clean. We all moved easily now, as we had several walks under our belts now, and everybody was determined.

I waited until I could show them where the soft moist soil had absorbed the weight of the lions, and we could finally see clearly how many and what age they were – approximately, of course.

My guests gathered around eagerly to see the pug marks. 'Here, see two or three adult lionesses walking, heading upstream . . . some yearling cubs . . . mmmmm . . . four at least, but you know cubs play and run around, so we can't be too certain right here,' I commented.

'Wow . . . There seem to be an awful lot of them. Are we safe doing this? Won't they object to being disturbed . . . I mean . . . there are more of them than us?' Concern being voiced.

'It's not that bad as long we respect their 'safe distance' and don't push them. Anyway, I'm sure they will take off before we see them, unless they decide to sleep somewhere nice and cool. You see, it depends on so many things, like how active they have been during the night and if they have eaten as well. They have been up all night and so are heading to sleep somewhere where they will not be disturbed. They have nothing to worry about, except elephants. Elephant chase lions, as they really don't like them at all. They eat their babies if they can!'

There was silence from my group as they absorbed this information. 'OK, let's go find them.' This was from one of the younger women. We hitched up our cameras and binoculars, put water bottles away, and I led the way.

The spoor was clear and consistent; they were following the river course inland. I had to be careful that we didn't walk into the thickets along the stream where rhino and buffalo lurked, as much as we would like to find them too.

Several times I paused to let the folk at the back catch up and ensured they changed places in the line as well. We were on a mission today, so I avoided chatting unnecessarily about birds and trees. We dodged a breeding herd of elephant as well and walked downwind to avoid disturbing them. We had a narrow 'pass' with a young teenage bull which was way behind the herd, and I had to gather my group behind some trees quickly and allow the elephant to wander past us unknowingly, just a few yards from our hiding place. My group were breathless with excitement!

Some bird alarm calls also made me pause to show them a slender mongoose foraging with a youngster trailing behind it. We carried on and then the lions split up.

I paused and explained what had happened. We followed the two adults and a scatter of cubs off to the west, and I stayed with the adults. The cubs, true to character, were playing and criss-crossed over the adults repeatedly. My concern was that the other group of lions (I did not know how many there were for sure) might lag behind, and we would walk on them suddenly, or this group might double back and see us following them, and they would disappear. Lions are unpredictable when on the move, and so we proceeded with caution. I had a couple of 'loo stops' too, as we had been going for two hours without a real break. My folk were still keen, and the sun was making the ambient temperature rise perceptibly. Sweaty faces and water bottles being drained were the result, and I knew we did not have too long before a halt would be called. I pulled off the trail under a shady tree and gave them an update on the 'spoor'. 'It's getting hotter now, and these cats will be settling shortly, I know,' I smiled at their eager, ruddy faces. 'We will give it another thirty minutes and then call it off. Is that OK with everybody?' I whispered. With the nods of agreement, I handed out some apples and three more bottles of water from my pack. Thank goodness, the extra water I always carried was heavy, but well worth the load. They chatted in whispers and then I heard a flock of guineafowl suddenly burst out of cover several hundred yards away, and to our far left. A few birds came whistling through the air at speed, but I could not see from where they had taken off.

'That could be the other group,' I said excitedly, 'or it could just be something else that's disturbed them.' Now a perceptible tension settled over us all as we set off again . . .

We followed an elephant trail, clear of leaves and much faster going for all of us and the lions too, of course. Hot ground and dry elephant-dung scent rose up in the heat as we silently made our way down the trail. My eyes scanned ahead, shady spots and dry leaves to be watched carefully. Then I saw the tip of a dark tail for a split second. It flickered up and down . . . a lion's tail! I stopped and turned around . . . 'LION,' I mouthed silently to my group. I indicated with my hand ahead. Silent 'ohs' came back and the message was passed down the line . . . huge, sweaty, red-faced smiles. I indicated they should follow me slowly and silently. There was no need to reiterate this, and we all crouched lower and inched forward. The light was dappled where we were, and I thankfully moved the group into full shade. The 'tail' was about 30 yards ahead, and I moved slowly until I could see the lion – in fact, lions! The whole group were prostrate in varying attitudes of lion-abandonment and slumber. I could not distinguish between the animals lying together as we were at a low angle, but it looked like a lot of lions! Checking to see that we were not about to disturb any animals in the foreground, I quietly beckoned my group to a point where they could see the lions asleep. Their faces were a study!

Exhilaration . . . fear . . . awe . . . disbelief – it was all there.

What a pleasure!

We were now about 25 yards from the nearest lion, flat out on its back, legs in the air, distended belly, finding relief in the shade, and under no pressure . . . I wanted to giggle to relieve the tension, I suppose. None of them had tried to take a photo, they were just totally mesmerised by the scene. We had found the mystical lions, and they didn't even know we were there. Their delight was a joy. Several of the cubs had flopped on or half on each other despite the heat, and a tangle of legs over faces and tails over bodies could be seen. Two of the three adult lionesses were close together, and the third, slightly away, right in front of us. I could not see any other animals that may have been lying apart from the lions we could see. The cubs were still spotted on their bellies and legs, and some of them still slightly blood encrusted, as they had killed something by the lakeshore during the night. Probably a zebra or a waterbuck. I did wonder where the pride males were, as there were another two lovely dark-maned male lions which patrolled a large section of the shoreline between my campsite and Tashinga, the National Park's station to the west. Perhaps this was one of their female groups too?

I looked around to see if there was a better spot with a better vantage point to enable us to watch them from further away, as some of my folk were really apprehensive. There was a termite mound a short distance back and off the trail, so I quietly waved them back. They all slowly, and with great care, crouching as low as they could, ghost walked back about fifteen yards, into another shady spot, and allowed me to pass them, and I told them what my plan was. 'Oh yes, that's a good idea,' was the collective response. We settled down on knees and bottoms, half hidden behind the mound and some branches, and watched the sleeping lions. My group were mesmerised. I dared not speak as any noise in the gathering stillness and heat of the day might have alerted the lions and they would have fled, and remembered it. Instead, we sat there for another fifteen minutes or so, and then I led my satisfied and creaky group away, back down the trail and out of lions' earshot.

What an adventure it was! Now we had a two-hour walk back to the vehicle.

The lunchtime was filled with happy chatter as each moment of that morning was relived, commented on by everybody, and then relived again. The elephants barely got a mention. Nobody could believe that the lions had not heard us at all and, as far as we knew, had woken up later, none the wiser.

CIVET CAT SPECIAL

Another funny incident occurred when on trail with Chris Sewell and his cousin, Peter Farrant, a doctor from Vaalwater, in South Africa.

The three of us were deep in the mountains, having traversed two mountain ranges and now we were in a river bed, high up on a hillside, towards the southern boundary of the park. Always reluctant to sleep in river beds, because of the danger of flash-floods, we had little choice, and it was September . . . rains were very unlikely. There was very little water around, and I had chosen a section where tall, thick grass and bushes grew right up against the bank, at least 40 m from the nearest rancid pool of scummy water, and out of the path of any possible water course.

We each had rigged our mosquito nets, and for once, I was in the middle of the group. Normally, I slept slightly apart from everybody, for safety reasons. We had enjoyed a flannel 'bath' at one of the side pools, having dug a hole in the sand next to the water, so the water had been filtered before we wiped ourselves down to try and get rid of the sweat from the day. Dinner had been well enjoyed and a cup of tea too . . . bed was welcome. It was about nine at night, and we were settling down in our sleeping bags, on a small, high-density mattress on a sheet of plastic – all tucked into a mosquito net. My net was dark green, allowing me to see through it at night, and Chris, who had been on several of my trips, had dyed his too. Peter's net was white.

We were just settling down, rustling and shuffling our way into our beds, settling heads on jackets or inflatable pillows. Chris was mumbling about something when I heard footsteps on the game trail, 7 metres away from us. 'Shhhh, Chris, there's something coming!' He didn't hear me. Carried on talking. 'Chris, shhh, there's something here!' . . . Still didn't hear me, but Peter did. The next second, something bolted through the grass straight towards us. I flicked on my Maglite. Rifle ready, facing forward. The grass was billowing forward towards us, and I shouted. Anything . . . loudly.

In a second, a smallish animal hit my backpack at the foot of my 'bed', bounced into the air, and landed on Peter, uttering a loud snarling growl. Peter bellowed in fright and kicked wildly with his legs, sending the poor creature skywards again! His white net billowing like a wild thing itself. His bellowing continued, and his net continued to have a life of its own. Then it was gone.

It was over in seconds.

It was a civet. The poor chap had been scared off the pathway, by who knows what (possibly our scent), and run helter-skelter straight into our camp.

We lay there, writhing with uncontrolled laughter, tears streaming down our faces, white and wide-eyed in the torchlight. It was hysterical, and the tension had to be assuaged. Then we all had to give our versions of the event, loud voices and more hysteria. Eventually, we settled down, still racked by bursts of laughter and giggles.

Eventually, silence . . . except for a rapid shuffling sound next to me – Peter's legs shaking with the adrenalin rush. More laughter and giggles. Sleep came late that night, when Orion had moved two hands-width across my view.

In the morning, the civet's spoor could be clearly seen, overlain by a leopard and Spotted hyenas as well. Poor chap, he had had the fright of his life, and so had we! Very fortunately, he hadn't released his scent gland contents over us; otherwise, we would have been a VERY odoriferous trio on trail!

Those wilderness trails were wonderful fun. Always an adventure, always the unexpected and memorable. Even now, nearly thirty years later, stories are retold and happy laughter resonates when some of us are gathered around a table, in Africa or on foreign shores.

***

THINGS THAT WENT 'BUMP' IN THE NIGHT

On another occasion, I was on a trail, and we had failed to get off the escarpment by sunset, and I had chosen to sleep on the sand in one of the many gulleys that led off the escarpment of the Matusadona. There were a small group of us, and as it was middle of the year, I figured that the chances of a sudden rainstorm were tiny. So after our normal dinner and tea, we had settled down, on the sand in what had been created by a waterfall, a small contained sandy basin about twenty feet wide with high, steep sides of the gulley. It was a perfect position for a night.

We all drifted off with the silver ball of the moon creating a dappled light through the leaves of the overhanging trees. It was a lovely evening.

A scattering of sand and gravel over me awoke me sometime in the night. The moon had traversed the night sky, so we lay in shadow now, with a sliver of silver over one corner. I lay listening. Crickets and the distant call of a fiery-necked nightjar . . . I smiled with contentment. Suddenly, more gravel fell around me. My ears strained to hear. There was a squeak high above me, a scrabbling sound and a higher series of frantic squeaky grunts. A cascade of gravel and a rattling sound thumped next to me. I sat up and stared. It was a porcupine! The poor chap was winded and just lay there for a moment. I stared at him, astonished. It gathered itself, sniffed the air around it, bristled a little, and then walked off grunting to itself quietly, as they do. I watched it find a way between the boulders of the stream; then I lay back and went back to sleep.

When I related the story to my fellow trekkers the next morning, they were a bit sceptical until I showed them the evidence – one broken quill and footprints!

SPRINGS AND THINGS

Later, when I was finally 'qualified' as a guide at Fothergill, I led my own walks and explored all the bays and creeks along the foothills, discovering secret springs and fern-covered fissures in the rock known only to birds and insects that clustered along the fringes of any moisture. I led small groups of guests along rocky ledges so we were above muddy patches, and we sat and watched pot-bellied rhinos wallow and grunt in bleary-eyed pleasure. Occasionally, a pair of klipspringer would appear, like shadows amongst the cliff vegetation, before spotting an incautious movement from my group, and with a wheezing snort of alarm, dash away up the ancient face of the cliffs, their fright giving them extra speed. I never saw them drinking and assumed they satisfied their moisture requirement from their browse diet.

Mongoose drank at these springs and, of course, small flocks of rock buntings, bulbuls, and other birds. Emerald-spotted doves always drank deep and long, before pausing to stare with black shiny eyes and rocketing away on cinnamon wings. Bushbuck would step delicately from cover, ears twitching, shiny wet noses and dark eyes watching. They would stoop briefly to suck the clear water and then just as quietly melt away into the sparse cover at the base of the cliffs.

Later, I would lead 'Wilderness trails' through the Matusadona and remember these small springs that never dried up even in the harshest years. At times, I had to lie on my side, next to a cleft rock with my orange plastic plate in my hand, arm fully extended into the crack to collect drops of the natural nectar, and carefully fill my old plastic fridge bottle that for years served as my water bottle.

I once filled five similar water bottles in this manner. It took me an hour and then had to refill mine again, as I used it to top-up those that had drunk half of their ration.

CHIKWENYA BULL

In 1981, Rob Fynn had successfully bid for the photographic concession for the 'old G camp', at the junction of the Sapi River and the Zambezi, on the boundary of Mana Pools. In 1982, John Stevens retired from National Parks and joined Rob and Sandy to help build and run the new camp, Chikwenya. Gael and I too had just joined the company to assist at Fothergill. It was a fine time to be a Zimbabwean, and the tourist industry had a great number of talented and energetic individuals who were to shape and move the industry to international heights. The next ten years were to be our best, and we ran with it.

The building of the camp was an adventure, and the Zambezi Valley was a 'wild' area then, with rhino, a common hazard on walks, and lions that were aggressive and elephants were thick in the jesse! Chikwenya was to become a milestone camp in the ecotourism system, and we enjoyed some unforgettable wildlife experiences in those wonderful early days. The Honourable Mrs Victoria Chitepo officially opened the camp in 1982, and we had rhino walking through the dining room every night. Now, only their ghosts walk through the Valley, and our memories keep them there.

Chikwenya was the 'new' camp to visit, and it enjoyed a notoriety for unbeatable game viewing, good food, and good fishing too. John and Nicci ran a good camp, and we enjoyed spending time with them when we could. Briar, their little girl, was four, and she was a pretty little blond elf, with big blue eyes. On the odd days that Gael and I had time off, it was my treat to come down from Fothergill Island and spend time in their camp and walk across the floodplains dodging rhino, cow elephants, and buffalo! Gael would not walk with me as she was still very wary of elephants from our 'honeymoon' scare.

We had another scare a few months later. I had finally managed to persuade her to come to a certain pan with me, whilst I photographed nyala, which, in the Zambezi Valley, are an antelope to get excited about.

She walked there peering behind every bush – all clear. We had been sitting on top of a tall anthill, carefully concealed in the bushes growing out of the mound when an elephant bull, cow, and calf appeared out of the jesse, about 500 m away.

Gael immediately reacted. Nudging me fearfully, she whispered loudly, 'They've seen us!'. Patiently, I calmed her fears, telling her they could not possibly see us as their eyesight was pretty limited at the best of times, let alone over this distance.

Minutes passed, the damned elephants walked deliberately straight towards 'our' mound. The cow and calf peeled off and went to the pan, 100 m from us. Whew, the tension lessened. The bull suddenly turned and started towards us. Gael was terrified. I climbed off the mound, leaving my rifle . . . and walked towards him, confident that he would make off. Gael, in tears by now, insisted I take the rifle. Crossly, I went back, collected it, and walked towards the bull, which, by now, had seen me. He paused. I walked on.

I started talking to him, telling him that he should leave NOW, as he was disturbing my bride and ruining my 'elephant rehab' effort . . . He 'stood tall', looked down at me through his tusks, and then charged.

I shouted and waved my arms. He kept coming. I bellowed loudly and threw my hat at him. In mid stride, he stepped over my hat and focused on me. By then, my rifle was off my shoulder, and I fired over his dusty forehead at almost point-blank range. Reloaded instantly, ready to kill him. He skidded to a halt within metres of me, paused, turned, and walked away. I stared at him, ready for a change of mind . . . Nothing, he carried on walking away.

I turned, and Gael was out of sight. Worried, I ran back to the mound. She was hunkered down, crying hysterically! I called her and tried to hold her. She couldn't believe it! I was alive. After some serious 'damage control' on my part, I managed to persuade her to walk back to the camp with me, taking a wide detour over the most open part of the plains, and the river bed. It was the last time we ever walked in the bush together.

Most of these stories have involved animals other than leopard and cheetah, for the obvious reasons that in those days, leopard were rarely seen on foot in the parks and areas that I worked in. Cheetah were, likewise, rarely seen by anyone working on foot anywhere!

Generally, sightings of leopard were brief and distant, even though their spoor and kills were found at intervals. One of my most interesting Mana Pool's leopard tales involved cubs and a shy female leopard.

A LEOPARD'S TAIL

I had a wonderful group of folk from the US with me, when I was doing a trip with John Stevens. We had been on a morning wander through the woodlands and were heading back to the camp. A lovely morning when the crisp clear air made a brisk walk to start the morning comfortable. Spoor of elephants, waterbuck, spotted hyenas, a solid line of pointed impala hooves, and all this covered by a web of the spikey three-toed prints of doves feeding in the silty sand had started our walks' 'points of interest'.

The calls of the starlings and doves of various kinds filled the woodland, and we walked diagonally across the floodplain towards the south-east from the camp, overlooking the Zambezi River. Mana has retained this magic even now, nearly thirty years later, but the woodland's character has changed, as it must, and more and more of the old trees are falling to create homes and food 'piles' for termites and other insects.

We spent a happy few hours tracking elephants and approaching them, shielded by shrubby trees and scrub so as not to disturb them. A spotted hyena pair walked determinedly past us at one point, seemingly unaware of us as we crouched still as logs in the weeds. Honey badgers also trotted by us, tails up like fluffy banners heading for home somewhere in the 'jesse'. Kudu and nyala lived in there as well, and ghosts of black rhino roamed free and untroubled now.

We had just found some crisp-fresh leopard spoor, and I was sure we were going to see the animal, so we had walked quickly (and silently) down a slight decline, searching the distance for the white-tail and markings of the leopard . . . as it trotted away from us. Nothing was seen.

It was there we had stopped for a break near the end of Long Pool, and watched the bristly snouts of the hippo as they snorted and cavorted with each other, and as the sun temperature rose, the crocodiles started to emerge and lie along the edge of the pool, pale mustard-coloured dinosaurs with tooth-filled jaws.

I was leaning against an old winterthorn, its massive trunk split near the base, with the rest of the group scattered around as we reviewed the morning and the fresh leopard spoor. The spoor had suddenly disappeared, and as the group were starting to lag, I had decided to let it go and take a break. We were chatting and passing around water bottles and fruit when I saw a short section of a python's tail protruding through the smaller crack in the tree base next to me. I put my water bottle down and peered disbelievingly at this tiny four-inch piece next to me. I followed it with my eyes into the tree and through a very narrow slit, turning my head, saw two tiny leopard cubs sitting blearily inside the hollow!

I quickly sat up, with rifle in hand, shushing everybody, and quietly pointed at the tail. Complete astonishment on everybody's face. 'Quick, take a peek and then let's get out of here . . . That leopard is right close by!'

'What is it?' they asked.

'A tiny leopard cub's tail! And there are two of them inside the base of this tree. Let's go quickly!'

To their credit, nobody tarried, and as we scuttled away guiltily, I looked back and, for a second, stared into the eyes of the female leopard. She had been up the tree all the time. As I lifted my arm to indicate where to look (she was sitting in the crook of two huge branches), she ran down the tree and disappeared into the dry weeds and uneven ground. Most of the group did not get even a glimpse of her. We stopped and waited for her to show herself, to no avail.

'She'll be back to move those cubs this afternoon. We compromised them, and she knows it well.'

That afternoon we went back, parked several hundred yards away, and from behind a screen of bushes, lay on our stomachs, with binoculars glued to our eyes, waiting for a glimpse of that female . . . and never saw her. She had already moved her babies!

It was not often we saw leopard in Mana. Partially I think because there was and still is no cover for them, thanks to the ever-present impala numbers that eat everything growing up to five feet in height, and because lion and hyena populations are high there, so competition is stiff. Baboons too are a threat to leopard, especially with little or no cover to take refuge in when dangerous numbers of baboons are prevalent.

Leopard were active at night as we heard them and found their spoor in the woodlands, but rarely did we see the Prince of Predators hunting in daylight there.

QUICK . . . THERE'RE THREE CHEETAHS!

I used to do a number of safaris for John Stevens in the early days of the 1980s and 1990s. John and Nicki had started a very successful safari business, and one of their flagship experiences was the 'mobile' tented camp that we would set up in Mana Pools, along the edge of the great Zambezi, at a designated site.

Sometimes John and I would do large groups together, as six people is a comfortable number to walk with, so we divided large parties between us. John and I have always got along very well together, and it's a great pleasure to work a safari as a team. The camps were always well organised, and I knew the staff personally, so it was a pleasure and a trip to look forward to. This trip, however, I was alone with a family of women. Mum and three daughters were in Zimbabwe, from England, and this safari was just one of the trips they were doing together. They were great fun and game for anything.

We were camped at one of the Mucheni sites where the riverbank had fallen away due to the rivers constant erosion, and so our camp was facing straight on to the river, towards Zambia. (This was long before the plethora of camps had been established on that side of the river.) It was peaceful paradise, and we had enjoyed some wonderful experiences. This was our last morning, and the aircraft was due to collect the family around midday.

The camp consisted of three separate small cottage tents, separated from each other by a few yards, under trees facing the river. The fire and 'main' area was merely where we had the camp chairs, under the deep shade of a sausage tree, which was conveniently in full leaf at this time of the year. The kitchen and staff area was well back and away from the riverfront so that we would not disturb the guests with cooking sounds and vehicle movement.

I slept in my own tent somewhere in this area.

Upstream of our spot, the riverbank was intact, and a lower river step created a massive plain, with a few gulleys, stands of *Vitiveria* grass and stands of winterthorn, and a few sausage trees as well.

A popular area for impala, waterbuck, warthogs, and, of course, elephants who would wander between the winterthorn, looking for pods or just grazing. It was about 500 yards from our camp, and just within sight.

Very early one morning, the alarm snorts of impala awoke me. I lay absorbing the sounds and smells of the pre-dawn, calculating where the sounds were and how far. The alarm sounds were a short distance away, upriver. I listened to the intensity of the alarms, trying to fathom which of the two main predator types it might be – lion or leopard? Difficult to tell, after a night of sleep and action . . . I dressed quickly, washed my face in the basin of warm water at my tent entrance, cursorily brushed my teeth, buckled on my ammunition belt, collected my rifle (always at my bed side when camping out), and walked away upriver. The pre-dawn darkness was intense, so I kept to the open areas between the trees. The sky was becoming light quickly, as it does in Africa, and soon I was able to see into the shadows too. A herd of elephant, a cow, several small adults, and two calves afoot foraged quietly around the twisted bole of a huge Zambezi fig, their silent forms choreographed in a slow ballet of feeding and shifting. Impala scattered on neat sharp hooves, only the drumming of the running hooves giving their shadowy forms substance. Numbers of doves and starlings were flooding the sound fields with morning calls and my footsteps led me to a point where I could see down across the plain, the alarm snorts of the impala and waterbuck no less in intensity.

My binoculars focused on several forms in the gathering dawn light. Impala – standing lean, heads fixed in unison towards a distant clump of grasses. I swept the 'glasses' backwards and forwards, scanning carefully everything that looked like an animal – nothing. 'Aahhh,' I thought, 'probably lions in the grass there.' I walked a bit closer, still several hundred yards from the isolated patch of grass. A flicker of movement caught my eyes on the far side of the clump – and there walked a cheetah! I stared, motionless. We rarely saw these lithe cats down here, and suddenly there was another, and another! Incredible. They strode into the field of view in my 'glasses'. Spotted, orange-eyed real sphinxes, with long white-tipped rudder tails waving casually from side to side as they walked side by side across the flood plain. They were well fed and did not look like they were likely to walk too far with full tummies. I silently ducked out of sight and walked directly away from them behind the screen of trees towards dead ground.

Once well clear of them, I ran as far as I could and then walked back to the camp.

The staff were up and about and were on their way with hot water to the guest tents. I walked with Mike to the farthest tent where he poured hot water into the canvas bucket outside the mother's tent, calling 'Good morning', as he did so. I waited a little out of breath for some response. A sleepy, 'Thank You', issued forth.

I had to get them out of bed very quickly, so I spoke out. 'Emily, there are three cheetah walking along the floodplain, and you have GOT to see them. PLEASE hurry, I need you out of there ASAP!'

Silence for a moment. 'Gavin, did you say cheetah? I thought you didn't get them here?'

'Hello, yes we do, but they are so very rarely seen. The girls are being woken, but I need to get you all there in the next few minutes, as I have no idea where they will disappear to . . .'. I paused, listening to various scrabbling sounds and mutterings. I walked away to the girls' tents nearby and repeated my urgings to them. They all caught the sense of the urgency, and within minutes, I had them all with me.

They had taken me at my word.

They were dressed in night attire, pale wafty short nightdresses of varying degrees of transparency, and boots! Two of them clutched equally wafty nightgowns about them, and Emily had on her safari shirt over her 'nightie'! Big smiles and tousled hair created delightful halos about them. I smiled back and cast an appreciative glance at them all, WOW . . . 'Well done, girls, that is fantastic! I think you lot should dress like that every day,' I laughed, and they giggled a little self-consciously, conscious of the morning chill and its effect on them. 'Let's go,' I said, still smiling, 'they are not far.' I spoke to them as we walked, their boots scraping on the hard ground every now and then. 'There are three of them, very likely males, and they may be closer now than when I saw them. The impala have been snorting alarms for the last hour, but it was a bit dark to see, so I had to wait a while for the light before I could see what it was.'

'So you have already been out, looking?'

'Yes, I had to see what it was that had everybody's attention out here.'

We walked fast until the top of the one of the river 'steps', and I slowed down, scanning the far brush line and open plain. I could still hear the impala and made my 'girls' listen until they could hear it clearly. The noise was closer, but I could not see any impala to give me direction. I scanned again and then saw a group of very tense and wide-eyed impala staring long-necked towards the river edge. There was a drop-off, some dead ground, and several old winterthorn silhouetted against the silver river behind. Yellow light touched the treetops now, and the floodplain was coming alive with birdsong, baboons, and other animals. Distant elephants browsed below the winterthorn, their trunks stretched out looking for the nutritious seedpods that had fallen during the night. A slight haze masked the scene like a soft grey filter, and Mana Pools started to come alive for a new day.

We stopped beneath a mahogany, and I pointed to where the impala were staring, giving the group a commentary on what was likely to be happening. My 'girls' were clustered together, focused now on the scene. I wished that I had a camera to record the picture of this charming group so absorbed in the scene unfolding in front of them. They were 'troopers', and I had thoroughly enjoyed my time with them. This cheetah experience was a real bonus for all of us.

They were sharing binoculars and so I handed mine over as well . . . and there they were. The cheetah ambled up the bank, emerging from the dead ground with caution and orange eyes, alert. They paused in the open 100 yards from our huddle and flopped down. Their graceful figures flattening out, only their tail tips and small heads showing clearly. They lay within close proximity of each other, their tail tips twitched and waved, each reflecting the owner's mood and disposition. The one animal was far more relaxed than the other two and lay flat on the ground, blending in with the other two. We stared and whispered soaking up the scene before us. I smoothed the sand for us all to sit down. They declined but crouched uncomfortably, knees bent behind a light screen of bushes.

The cheetah appeared not to see us, fortunately, as I was certain they would take off if they knew we were there.

After ten minutes, Emily said in a strangled whisper, 'Somebody help me. I cannot stand up.' I pulled her up gently, and she grimaced with pain, massaging her knees. 'Sorry, but I cannot sit like that any more.' I moved her slowly behind a tree trunk in deep shade. 'No problem,' I smiled, 'I can't either.'

The cheetah were relaxed now, resting with their eyes closed, heads propped up as only a cheetah can be, even their tail-tips were barely twitching now. 'OK, shall we leave them?' I whispered.

Nods of assent, and we quietly pulled back, using the dead ground again to hide us.

That afternoon Emily's group left Mana Pools forever, but they left lasting memories with me. The image I have of the single file of women in short nightdresses and safari boots wending their way carefully (with no snags) through the Mana scrub and across the floodplain behind me, with elephants and the Zambezi River as a back drop will remain forever. What a sight . . . What a finale!

UNEXPECTED COMPANY AT MY BEDSIDE

After independence in 1980, Zimbabwe was flooded with NGOs and foreigners all responding to the call of the UN to help rebuild the country. Some of these were sincere and did some great things, and others were hyenas, scavenging what they could. One of the initiatives was to find oil in the country, as the country had some of the largest coal reserves in Africa, and therefore the possibility of oil could not be ruled out. I accepted the task of accompanying one of the geo-survey teams into the Zambezi Valley, to ensure they did not get eaten by anything and to establish a temporary base from which they (and their helicopter) could operate.

I set up a base camp at Nyakasanga Bridge, on the road into Mana Pools where there was a well and a pump. The Ruckomechi River was a broad expanse of sand, dotted with ancient winterthorn trees and as the dry season progressed, the water level below the sand dropped further and the elephant bulls had to find alternative water sources or walk down to the Zambezi River itself, many, many kilometres downstream. My camp was set up in an open patch of level ground, and my staff had done well in setting up the tents for the two geologists (one Zimbabwean and one American), and the pilot of the helicopter. I did not have a tent, preferring to sleep in my mosquito net under a 'jesse' bush, on a stretcher, in my bedroll. This I was used to and slept well, in the fresh air, protected from predators' attentions by the thick bush around me. I had found a huge bush, not far from the camp, and a buffalo had created a little 'cave' inside the bush, under the sheltering branches. So, I cleared out the buffalo dung, scraped fresh dry leaves over the area, and set up my bed, under my mosquito net. I did a lot of wilderness trails in those days and had a custom-made net, which was as long as my bedroll and hung off a parachute cord stretched between two points, like a tree or a stick I buried in the ground.

That evening, I retired to bed after a shower and a good dinner around the fire.

I had finally settled down and was drifting off to a satisfied sleep when I heard the steady plod of heavy footsteps and knew the old buffalo was about to get a shock! I saw him stop a few paces from the entrance to his 'jesse' cave, sniff loudly, jerk his head up, and he galloped noisily off, his great hooves making quite a noise as they faded into the night . . . a cloud of dust drifted over me, and I smiled. 'Sorry, old chap, I'll only be here for a few days.' Sleep claimed me, and I was gone.

Lion roars woke me a couple of hours later – nothing close by, but over the dry river somewhere . . . I lay and listened and hoped that the old buffalo had not become a meal for the lions calling. As I pondered on this, listening to the rhythmic grunts at the end of the roar, I heard the soft sound of padded feet – many of them coming towards me from over my left shoulder, beyond my bush. I knew they were lions – and hurrying too. I lay still and tried to slow my heartbeat down . . . 'Calm down,' my inner voice said, 'you have slept out with lions so many times . . . what's different here?' I half raised myself so that I could see out of the entrance better in the very pale light of the clear night sky. I saw sloped backs, tails and tips of tails . . . the whole pride walked past my hideout at a pace. They were hurrying to join the owner of the roar over the river. I could not count the animals, but at least, eight lions walked past then. They hurried off and away.

I lay back quietly and smiled. It was fun to be the 'observer' for a change, and not the 'seen'. All was quiet, and the adrenalin that flowed into my system was absorbed and left me at peace but alert to sounds. Crickets sounded loud, and a bat squeaked repeatedly as it hunted around the edges of the jesse. Lion roared again, but muted by distance and direction. The group were calling now as they walked towards the others, their voices at uneven pitches.

Suddenly, I heard footsteps again, coming from behind me . . . soft feet, but fewer, and then leaves scuffed right behind me. I turned in a flash, my hand on my big Maglight . . . and the bushes moved behind my head. I turned on the light as a young lioness's face was coming around the bundles of stems next to my head. For a nano second, she was transfixed in my beam . . . her iris responded, it was golden, flecked with tiny brown dots, and it contracted in the light. Her whiskers were almost white, the roots black, and bedded in her smooth muzzle, nose pink and wet, with a little dust and tiny bits of leaf and smooth, wet thin lips. For a moment in time, she stood a breath away from me, and then with a 'woof', she disappeared. She had a companion. I had turned the torch on just for a second, and my eyes took a moment to adjust.

I heard movement to the side and sat up quietly. There were two lionesses in the silver light of the night, staring at me from the front of my 'cave', necks stretched out, frightened, stiff legged, and ready to bolt in a second.

I spoke to them. 'Sorry, girls . . . but you should have walked around the bush.' They paused a second longer and then trotted off, melting into the night for good. 'Whew . . . ,' I breathed, 'that was amazing!' Even though this incident occurred so many years ago, I remember so well, the lionesses' eye, its colour, and the iris contracting instantly in the brief blinding flash of my torch.

The remainder of the night was peaceful, as were the following nights that I was under my bush. White-tailed mongoose, genet, and the odd civet were my neighbours then, and they did nothing to disturb my rest.

CAREFUL, THERE'S A CROCODILE HERE!

It was during this escapade in the Valley with the oil-prospecting crew that I had another interesting find. We had flown down into the Chewore and were somewhere towards the escarpment looking for river cuttings that would expose the 'scarp' and 'dip' of the rock strata. 'Mike,' the American fellow, pointed downwards to the pilot and spoke into his microphone, 'Looks promising, down there . . . Can we land somewhere close?' The pilot looked down scanning the area, the whine of the turbo in the Jetranger's engines had deafened all of us; he nodded and started to descend. A pride of lions had been resting in the shade near a stream, and they watched us suspiciously for a few moments before trotting off, ears back, into the surrounding brush. Massive sandstone cliffs had been sliced open by water and time, and the raw earth face was on the other side. It was these that had attracted Mike's attention. We climbed out of the helicopter, I collected my rifle, and the three of us wandered over to the cliff. The pilot stayed with his machine.

Narrow bands of low-grade coal were not uncommon finds here, and we had heard the excitement from the American fellow a few times and quietly threatened him with dire consequences if he did find oil – the last thing any of us wanted was a wretched oil find in the Valley.

Anyway, Mike and the Zimbabwean fellow, Greg I think his name was, pottered about taking Polaroid photos which they carefully annotated and filed, and I watched the scrub in case the lions returned and objected. I scanned the towering cliffs, being a keen birder, as it was a great place for a raptor nest site. It turned out to be a new record site for a Taita falcon, and coincidentally, a black stork was nesting there too. But I only found those a while later.

It was hot, and eventually, Mike and Greg had tired of their 'prospecting' and wandered over to the stream that flowed at the base of the cliffs. The under-cut of the water had cut deeply into the foot of the cliff, creating a deep shelf that went in about nine feet or so. I was a little way behind them, when they stripped off and were looking for a deeper spot in the stream that would cover their torsos, so they could cool down. The pilot had brought out our lunch and was carrying the box towards us, to the cool shade of the cliff. I wandered over, grinning at the two geologists, comparing white, very un-muscly bodies and abusing each other verbally. Suddenly, I noticed the impression of a medium-sized crocodile in the sand! 'Hey, guys . . . there's a crocodile here!' They stopped and looked at me, expecting me to be making fun of them. I was deadly serious. 'Look here . . . see . . . the belly scale marks and the tail . . . here are the feet . . . see the back foot is webbed.' They moved away quickly.

'It's OK,' I went on, 'just don't lie down where you can't see the bottom . . . this fellow is about five or six foot long. Enough to give you a bad bite and whip off a hand or your whatsit . . .'

'Thanks,' they exclaimed. 'Forget swimming . . . Are you sure?'

Said I, 'That's why I'm here . . . to look after you lot and stop you feeding the wildlife down here . . .' I smiled at them. 'Splash water on yourselves by all means, just don't get creative.' We hunted around and could not find the crocodile at all . . . but he had been there very recently, and so the fellows just had a splash-bath, and at least a cold beer! I was astonished at finding the crocodile so far up in the escarpment, in shallow water, where clearly he was 'at home', and well fed, judging from the width of his belly mark. It was a good lesson for me, as I had often swum in mountain pools at the top of the Matusadona escarpment.

LIONS IN MANA POOLS

I was used to doing a lot of freelance guiding for a couple of operators, and it was during a camping and canoeing trip that I had a 'close' encounter with a big lion. We were camped at Chessa campsite, below the Nyamepi public camp area, and I had three guests with me. A single woman and a married couple from the USA.

Our tents were placed along the edge of the river facing Zambia, as usual, and my small tent had been placed at the far end of the camp, where the staff knew I preferred to be, away from any noise and with a little privacy.

During a camping and canoeing trip, we only spent one night at each spot before moving the next day. It was a simple trip and one that I enjoyed from time to time, as the river is a wonderful experience, and my guests were fun to be with.

Later that evening, the local lion pride were busy harassing a couple of old buffalo bulls on the flood plain near the camp, when the bulls decided to run through the camp and escape on to an island right across the narrow channel over which the camp was placed. They did so with much snorting, and galloping hooves and noise. The lions tried to follow them, and eventually got bored with the whole exercise and gave up.

I had watched some of the chase through the gauze of my tent and had seen two of the lions involved. They were a pair that I had seen a few times further down the floodplain, beyond the Chiruwe mouth. The lioness with them slumped down at the river edge and lay there staring at the buffalo which had wandered off to the far side of the island and stood watching the lions with red-eyed disdain.

I went back and lay down, shuffling into my sleeping bag in the limited room of the tent. I heard footsteps and then a heavy body lay on my thighs and legs . . . through the tent.

A REALLY heavy body . . . I lay pinned and unbreathing . . . It was a lion. I had heard him grunt as he flopped down. I didn't move – actually, I couldn't move. I lay there, with a curious elation in me. I was lying next to, touching . . . almost . . . a big male lion, and it was tremendously exciting! He was so warm and solid, and my toes were losing circulation. He shifted his elbow slightly, shifting his weight a little, it was between my knees. The temptation to want to stroke him through the tent was almost unbearable. I wanted to see him. Impossible. I lay there, a silent witness to this wonderful animal as he contemplated the evening, and probably his companions.

It was possibly a mere five minutes, or so when he grunted again and stood, breathing heavily and the soft scrunch of sand next to me receded as he walked out of my 'arena'. He was gone. My magic moment with this king of the predators was over . . . but it's with me still. Some twenty years later! I have since handled adult lions and marvelled at their smooth strength and lines, their oily coats, massive paws and scimitar claws, and watched them in action, fighting, mating, and killing. There are few sights more awe-inspiring than a big male lion walking towards or charging you on foot. It's a moment you never forget.

THE RUKOMECHI LIONS

Talking about lions always evokes sharp memories, I suppose, because the incidents past were tinged with a larger dose of adrenalin and therefore remain clearer in the memory.

I was with guests of my own down at Rukomechi Camp, on the Zambezi River, on the border of Mana Pool's National Park, Zimbabwe. Rukomechi is still there, having weathered two decades of rainy seasons, floods, and tragedy as well as unique wildlife sightings.

Conservation Travel had sent me a Canadian guest, Jon, Elizabeth, his wife, and his young daughter, Leonie, for their first African safari. He was very keen to collect as many images of Africa – quality images – as possible. Emphasis on 'quality images'. Our first morning drive from the camp had taken us down 'Ambush Alley', an area well known to the camp guides where elephant herds in the evening would make life exciting for late game-drive vehicles. The fever berry crotons were thick here and the sandy track wound between these dense bushes and the elephant cows would scream and trumpet loudly as the vehicles pass them, scaring everybody in the vehicle and trying young trainee guides. 'Fox-terrier leg' was a common syndrome for young guides, in those days, when the post-elephant encounter would leave them with shaky legs!

We had driven down through the crotons towards the river and the large flood plain, where the river step was accessible. It was always productive, and herds of waterbuck frequented the lower (newer) floodplain where the lush grass and river provided a day's good grazing. Hippo and zebra were also often here. The upper (older) flood plain was a winterthorn woodland, dotted with thickets of jesse and gulleys of Vitiveria spp. grass, which provided good cover for lion, leopard, honey badgers, buffalo – in fact, anything that wanted to hide! What a lovely morning!

As we entered the woodland, I could see waterbuck staring at something on the far left of us, and there was a pair of lion walking purposefully along the lower step. Fantastic – lions on our first drive. I took the lower step track, hoping to get close to the lions in the vehicle for photography. Jon was really excited. 'Can we stop and photograph them?' he asked, eyes shining. 'Of course, let's just see where they are going, shall we?' I answered. 'Let's drive on a bit and then we can get out and stalk them carefully, before they go to cover.' The lions had paused in the shade of a clump of *Vitiveria*, but we could not get too close to them due to the terrain.

I stopped the car near the edge of the steep bank, which was the foot of the river step.

We climbed out. I briefed them all on the protocols of walking here with dangerous animals, and particularly, lions. Jon and his wife appeared totally nonchalant about it all, and the daughter was smiling and relaxed. 'OK, great,' I thought. I laid out our plan of action. 'OK, we are going to walk up the bank here, to get above the lions, then see how they are with us above them, before we collect images. OK?' I looked at Jon and his wife. Yup, all good.

Our walk took us up the bank about 100 yards from the lions, away from them and then along the top of the bank, crossing from the lions right to their left. Slowly, and keeping some cover between us, we made our way across until we had a good view of them. We stopped, and Jon set up his tripod. Took a few shots. The lions got up and walked away from us and parallel to the step. We walked on. The lions stopped again . . . watching us. We were still about 100 yards away. I stopped the group, and we talked quietly about the lions, Jon was taking photos. The lions started walking towards us, following a faint game trail which was leading them up to the step on the same level as us. The light was not right for photos. I wanted Jon to photograph them walking towards us with the light on their shoulders, but the angle was not good, so we started to walk back to get the angle right. The lions started trotting, watching us closely.

I stopped and found a large Capparis bush growing on the edge of the slope, paused, and realised the lions were coming for us! The lioness had, in fact, broken off to the left and was walking towards the Land Rover parked about eighty yards away. The lion was coming for us. He came straight up the slope and walked straight towards me. I warned the family that the lion was going to try us, so we backed up towards the Capparis bush and waited. Note that through all of this time, nobody has said a word, except Jon, who tried to stop, set up his tripod, and take a photo of the lion approaching us – tempting, I agree, but it wasn't the time to do it.

The lion was now growling ominously and hunched his shoulders aggressively at me. I talked to him. I told him he was being tiresome, and we were not in his way. He growled more loudly, staring at me. I had chambered a soft-nosed bullet when they had first shown interest in us and was prepared to shoot him, as a last defence. However, negotiation was first in my mind right then but, admittedly, receding slowly.

Jon was taking a photo over my shoulder. The lion didn't like it at all and snarled loudly and took a step towards me. I shouted at him . . . he paused. I had an idea. 'Jon, I want you to help Elizabeth down the slope behind the bush, and then Leonie, and then wait for me. I will come down last. This lion is not going to let us move anywhere else.' He took one more photo (which really got the 'lion's' turbo' going) and then did as I had asked. When he was down the bank behind the bush, he called out to me, and I slowly retreated, rifle at the ready. The lion stalked me as I moved back, until I slid down the bank, and he charged the spot where I had been a moment before! I now lay against the bank, rifle levelled at the lion, crouched just above me. I was on the point of shooting him when he calmed down and crouched. He watched us creep away from the slope and sat there. 'Lead us towards the vehicle, Jon,' I called out. 'There's another lion here,' he answered. We were thirty yards away from the bank now, and I turned around to see the lioness lying near the vehicle, a nasty look on her face, ears back, tail straight out behind her. Oh, dear. She lay facing us, clearly intent on obstructing us. I scanned the top of the bank; the lion was still there, but relatively calm now and casually watching us.

I looked at the lioness. She was nasty. We had no alternative. 'OK, we are going to call her bluff,' I said. No answer. I looked at them – all smiles, even the daughter. 'Amazing,' I thought, most people would be dying of fright or making a fuss, but these guys, not a peep. I told them all to bunch behind me, and we walked straight towards the crouching, snarling lioness. She was the epitome of nasty. Flat crouch, ears flat against her flat head, eyes burning yellow, boring straight through mine . . . her upper lip drawn back, teeth slightly yellow and snarling, she was in full 'turbo' as we used to say of a lion's growl. I carried on walking, straight towards her, everybody tight behind me. The lioness seemed to hesitate, glanced sideways towards the male, and then did the unexpected. She bolted sideways. I had my rifle in my shoulder anyway, and I tracked her, my foresight on her right shoulder where the heavy bullet would shatter her heart in a blind second if she changed her mind.

She trotted away without looking back, her ears angled back towards us, off to join the male who had walked away whilst we had approached the female.

So she had lost courage perhaps when she had seen the male lose interest in us, perhaps?

I have been confronted by a number of lions over the years since then, but rarely had anything like that intensity of aggression, from a casual encounter.

We reached the Land Rover, and I helped them in, before unloading my rifle and offering them something to drink.

Absolutely not a sound from any of them!

At brunch that morning, there's always discussion on what has been seen that morning, I expected my guests to tell everyone about our rather tense incident with the lion, but no, they just said they had had an interesting morning with lions!

When I recounted the story after brunch, one of the guides said he had a similar but not as drastic an incident with that particular lion, and he wished I had shot him. 'You would have done us all a favour, Gavin!'

That lion lived for several years, I know and then disappeared one season, and I hope his fierce spirit still roams the woodlands of the Zambezi Valley.

LIONESSES AND THEIR CUBS

The Matusadona features a lot in my early career, and it was a wonderful area to operate in. The mountains, the lake, and the flat foothills were a hugely diverse area to operate in and exercised many skills that we had to refine as guides. There was such an abundance of big game that every drive or walk had something of interest for guests and myself too. Today when I talk to young guides, I try and instill in them the privilege they have in Zimbabwe and elsewhere in Africa of being out in the bush, where every day is a learning opportunity.

Lions were always a quest for people on walks, and we would spend hours tracking them and black rhino too.

I was walking with two British army officers and their four youngsters, between nine and thirteen years of age. The two eldest were boys and full of mischief. Before we had started on the walk, I had given a serious briefing about the issues of walking with kids and the dads were in complete agreement. So we had set off. Driving down to an area known for good general plains game, I had hoped that we would thereby avoid any problem encounters. It was an area on the Matusadona shoreline, scrubby on the ridges and open shorelines where we would have a great view across the parallel ridges and be able to spot game from a way off. It was not to be!

We had scarcely gone a hundred yards when I found lion spoor – fresh. It was not just lion spoor, but a whole pride PLUS small cubs! I was remarking that it would be a good idea to turn back and walk somewhere else when a flock of guineafowl flushed some distance ahead of us. They had been flushed by the lions, I was sure. The dads wanted to see lions, so I just said they had to hold on to the kids, as young cubs spelt trouble if we bumped into them. We stayed very close together and walked on. We were on the top of a ridge, a bit scrubby, but essentially well grassed and fairly open. I scanned the front of us carefully –

nothing. We carried on and the guineafowl were making a huge din, and now I could see them some way ahead of us, sitting untidily in a dead tree, looking down at the ground, which was out of our sight.

We stopped and crouched down. I scanned again using binoculars, but the ground fell away about 150 yards ahead of us, down a steep bank to the lake shore. The lions were down near the water, I presumed, at the end of the ridge we were walking on. That meant they had to come back past us! I relayed this to the dads. Everybody was very quiet. I spotted some yearling lions on our left side, walking back towards our position but below us on the lakeshore. Good. They would eventually pass below us along the edge of the water, and we would still be on the top of the ridge, and the little wind was in our favour. Phew.

I briefed everybody on our strategy. We were going to hide in some bushes and watch the lions walk past, where we could see and not be seen! I placed everybody in a position behind some thick bushes where the ground fell away a little, allowing us all full visual of the lakeshore on the left. We would stay in hiding until the lions had gone past and then walk away to the other side of the ridge, keeping out of sight.

We didn't have long to wait. There they came. Three playful yearlings, still spotted and clumsy chasing each other and running around between three lionesses and a young male lion. Bringing up the rear was a large lioness with five very young cubs which were gamely trotting along behind their mother and tripping over the driftwood and debris on the waterline. Their soft growls and whines came to me in the still air. We watched with awe as they ambled past us. What a sight! Their tawny coats burnished in the morning light, large pale brown spots on the bellies of the three lionesses, denoting that they were not old, but mature animals. The lion was probably a sibling, with a tufty mane. It couldn't have worked better! I looked at one of the men. His eyes were fixed on the lions, a half smile around his mouth. They were possibly fifty yards from us, down the slope and totally unaware of us. The kids watched silently, eyes big.

The lions were past us now, and so I waited a moment before moving out and into the open slowly. The men followed me with the little girls, and the one boy too. The other youngster was behind them. They smiled at me in huge appreciation for the success of our ruse and then I heard the soft growl! I stepped around the men, and the second boy was coming back into the open – he looked sheepish!

'Quick, they are coming. Stand behind me, they will come through here now!' The men didn't need a second urging, they were army officers who understood action. I cocked my rifle and checked the load as it was chambered. Soft-nosed.

'The lionesses saw Tim . . . didn't they?' I indicated the boy, and he looked down. His father grabbed him and pulled him into the group. 'Is that true?'

It was true because at that second, there was a rush and two lionesses burst around the small bush to our right and, snarling, loudly rushed in. I stepped forward and shouted at them. They skidded to a halt, just yards from us, tearing at the ground and grass. A third one came round another bush. 'STAND STILL . . . STAND STILL,' I shouted. Both for the people and the lions. The lionesses backed off and came again. This time closer still – just a few steps from me. There was hate and anger in their eyes. Their beautifully muscled bodies taut with fight, tails slashing sideways with each growl, tearing at the grass, working themselves into a frenzy that could be fatal. I talked to them now, lowering my voice . . . telling them silly things . . . but my rifle stayed in my shoulder, finger ready to touch the trigger in a second. They broke off again, and I stepped back a pace. One came back again, sneaking in from the side, the others were still there in support – out of sight – I had the rifle sighted on her eyes and speckled nose. She snarled some more and backed off a tad. I stepped forward a pace still talking to her. A second lioness came through growling now, and then looked behind her, growled some more, and then backed off and trotted away. The others had vanished.

I stayed where I was, scanning the bushes and sides. 'Is everybody OK?'

'Yes, we are fine. Have they gone?'

'I think so. Just stay where you are and watch your flanks!' I answered.

I took a few paces forwards and nothing happened. Took a few more into the open and scanned around in front and to the sides – not a lion to be seen. I beckoned them to follow me, and we stumbled down to the edge of the bank so we could see further along the shoreline. Nothing. I used my binoculars – still nothing. They had vanished.

I turned back to my group who were staring at me a little apprehensively. 'Well, that was an experience for you to remember. Did you see how close they came! Man, they were angry. Those 'girls' were REALLY ticked off with us!'

'Tim, you disobeyed my instructions, didn't you?' I stared at him. His father would give him a severe dressing down later, I knew. 'I just wanted to see them again, and she was looking as I peeked over the bushes.' He was a little cocky. A little contrition would have been better. 'Well, that wasn't smart. You see, lions are predators and are designed for speed and killing. Their eyesight and sixth sense is remarkable. She may have guessed something was wrong, which was why she looked back right then.' I paused, 'You see how quick she was? They must have covered a hundred yards in seconds to get here so quickly. We'll have a look now when we walk back.'

'You mean we have to walk past them?' Deep concern from one of the girls. 'Well, I don't think they will be there. They also got a big fright and so will have gone off somewhere out of sight from us, but don't worry, we'll take care. You were all very good, by the way.' This to the men and their little girls. 'A lion charge is a damn scary thing.'

'How did you hear them coming? If you hadn't, it could have been tickets for us.' 'Well, yes,' I answered slowly, 'it might have meant a dead or wounded lion and a badly chewed guide and guests, because they would have hit me first and then you! They work each other up into a fury and then it's hard to stop them without shooting.'

'Gavin, what did you say to them? I mean, does it make sense?'

'No, I had to shout and be angry, because they were giving me the same vibe. Then, we could not back down to them, so I just spoke more gently to try and defuse their intensity. It doesn't always work, especially with small cubs, you see. I have found that the smaller the cubs, the more intense the anger or protection response. That's why I made sure you were all clear before we carried on earlier when I saw how small the cubs' spoor was.'

We walked back to the vehicle, following the lion spoor on the sandy waterline. We could see clearly where the lionesses had started their charge back to intimidate us. It was just over a hundred metres and very clear, with immense strides dug deep into the sand. The cubs had scattered and then later regrouped, and the pride had gone inland.

We walked along the open beach area. We had had enough excitement for one day!

LEOPARDS AND LIONS AT SAUSAGE TREE

It is not often that one sees lion and leopard in the same proximity with a happy ending. Lions will chase and kill the spotted cat when they can. Lions will steal leopard kills when they find them in a tree or under a bush, but it is commonly the slim, lighter lionesses which can climb trees with a degree of agility, and not the big males, who will stand at the base of the tree and hungrily eye a kill or growl and snarl at a leopard unfortunate enough to have been caught sleeping in a tree.

I was on safari in the Lower Zambezi National Park, with a pair of English guests who had done several safaris with me. We were enjoying an afternoon drive which had started really well with a lucky find, a broadbill displaying in the shade of a huge mahogany tree. The afternoon had been very successful with a variety of great game sightings, and then a great sundowner, overlooking the broad sweep of the Zambezi. Our guide was an enthusiastic young man, who had infused the drive with fun and passion, a great combination. We were just discussing the prospects for the drive home and the possibility of seeing a leopard in the riverine forest areas or the lovely winterthorn forest. Off we went, the spotlight carving a brief shaft of light from side to side, our heads moving from side to side in synchrony with the light. We had found a genet, that silent, lithe carnivore sitting cat-like with feet folded under its chest, watching the track from the top of a termite mound. We avoided shining the light directly on it, and marvelled at the colouring and white spots on its face through binoculars. Further on, a pair of rubies flashed briefly in the light high up in the canopy of a winterthorn, a lesser bushbaby. Bushbabies' eyes glow a brilliant red in the light. We stopped and searched for the little grey ghost amongst the branches – seeing it briefly before it vanished in a jump out of the light. We carried on, something had run across the track just before we reached that spot, and a cloud of fine dust hung in the air . . . with just a whisper of a stir . . . could have been any number of creatures.

We rounded a corner, the vehicle lights illuminating the tree trunks and mass of creepers hanging off a tree on the right. I spotted an impala ram standing in the shadows on the left, and the vehicle slowed as the corner was very 'tight'. Suddenly, there was a light shadow, and a leopard sprang from behind the impala, hitting it on the neck, and the two of them were there, rolling into the dusty track in a flurry of bleats, kicking legs, dust, leopards' tail and more obscuring dust.

We stopped, throwing us all forward off the seats. Dawn and Jeremy had slid on to the floor, and now joined me standing behind the cab.

We stared transfixed, watching this life-and-death struggle. The dust cleared slowly. There was a leopard with a throat-hold on a large impala ram. We stared . . . the leopard was sitting facing left, the impala was down, its head muzzled upwards, throat firmly in the leopards' jaws . . . and behind this desperate duo was another leopard, standing, watching! Slightly smaller, this animal could have been a female or a large cub. I wasn't sure. It wasn't relevant right then. I quickly gestured to the second leopard and Jeremy and Dawn nodded in acknowledgement, they had seen it too. Silence had descended with the guide turning off the engine. The blanket of the night lay on us, with only the headlights focused on the scene in front of us. It was like a macabre play, and the actors were real.

Suddenly the smaller leopard vanished. Not a sound was to be heard, and the leopard holding the impala, tightened its grip, as the impala's legs started to cycle. It was nearing the end.

A big male lion walked on to the scene!

We stared, open mouthed – shocked by the appearance of the big cat, and for the impending tragedy that was imminent. The lion was going to kill the leopard.

The lion was behind the leopard, stalking the cat on silent feet, its eyes fiercely focused, body taut, and shoulders hunched for the pounce. It was barely six feet away from the leopard's tail. A sixth sense warned the leopard on the impala, and it leapt over the impala still with the antelope in its jaws. On seeing the lion, which had stopped motionless, the leopard dropped the impala and fled up the nearest tree. The impala fell on the ground, making gurgling noises, its head flopping sideways. The lion watched the leopard fleetingly before advancing on the doomed impala and pinning it down with a large paw. The lion looked up the tree and stared at the leopard which was by now at least forty safe feet up the tree! Only the sound of loose leaves and bark falling down could be heard.

We were flabbergasted! What a drama to witness! The lion still held the impala which had recovered pretty well by now and was struggling under the lion's paw. The lion rather absent-mindedly then dispatched the hapless antelope with a strong neck bite, and in short order, the impala's life was over. Finally.

The next morning, we returned to the scene to find the lion with a half-eaten impala, under the same tree, with the leopard which was balancing way up on a thin branch trying to wash itself. Only the following afternoon did that lion leave and the leopard finally get away. Lucky leopard!

Safaris today have not lost their lustre, and the industry, for that is what it is now is still as exuberant as it ever was. All that has changed is the scope and variety of the visitors who venture onto our shores. I no longer live in Zimbabwe, but after a spell of seven and a half years in Botswana working with a well-known safari operator, we moved to South Africa. My safari life has changed somewhat, driven by time and circumstances but there is still a great thrill to waking up in the bush, somewhere between South Africa and Ethiopia and knowing that the day ahead promises to be different from yesterday, each day is an adventure.

Lightning Source UK Ltd.
Milton Keynes UK
UKIC01n2320030615
252862UK00007B/60